PASTA

ENTERTAINING

PASTA

ENTERTAINING

FABULOUS IDEAS FOR
SPECIAL OCCASION DISHES

Linda Fraser

Sebastian Kelly

This edition published in 1998 by Sebastian Kelly

© Anness Publishing Limited 1998

Produced by Anness Publishing Limited
Hermes House, 88–89 Blackfriars Road, London SE1 8HA

ISBN 1 84081 028 9

Publisher: Joanna Lorenz
Senior Cookery Editor: Linda Fraser
Cookery Editors: Rosemary Wilkinson, Linda Doeser
Copy Editor: Val Barrett
Designers: Bill Mason, Siân Keogh
Illustrator: Anna Koska

Recipes: Catherine Atkinson, Carla Capalbo, Maxine Clark, Roz Denny, Christine France,
Sarah Gates, Shirley Gill, Norma MacMillan, Sue Maggs, Elizabeth Martin, Annie Nichols,
Jenny Stacy, Liz Trigg, Laura Washburn, Steven Wheeler
Photographs: Karl Adamson, Edward Allwright, David Armstrong, Steve Baxter, Jo Brewer,
James Duncan, Michelle Garrett, Amanda Heywood, Patrick McLeavey, Michael Michaels
Stylists: Madeleine Brehaut, Jo Brewer, Carla Capalbo, Michelle Garrett, Hilary Guy,
Amanda Heywood, Patrick McLeavey, Blake Minton, Kirsty Rawlings, Elizabeth Wolf-Cohen
Food for Photography: Wendy Lee, Lucy McKelvie, Jane Stevenson, Elizabeth Wolf-Cohen

Front Cover: Lisa Tai, Designer; Tom Odulate, Photographer;
Helen Trent, Stylist; Lucy McKelvie, Home Economist

Previously published as part of a larger compendium, *Best-Ever Pasta*

Printed in Hong Kong/China

1 3 5 7 9 10 8 6 4 2

NOTE
Medium eggs should be used unless otherwise stated.

CONTENTS

Introduction

Pasta is perfect for entertaining. Everybody loves it, and most dishes can be prepared and cooked easily and quickly, allowing you to spend time with your guests, rather than isolated in the kitchen. There are dishes here for all tastes, from Italian classics, such as Tagliatelle with Prosciutto and Parmesan to vegetarian specialties, such as Leek and Chèvre Lasagne.

The book begins with an introduction to the main types of pasta, a guide to useful sauces and pastes, and step-by-step instructions for making fresh homemade pasta. The recipes are divided into six chapters: Soups, Fish & Shellfish Dishes, Meat & Poultry Dishes, Vegetarian Dishes, Salads, and Desserts. The easy-to-follow-recipes are superbly illustrated in color, and hints and tips throughout the book provide further information and suggestions.

Pasta is wonderfully versatile and goes well with almost all other ingredients, including meat, poultry, fish, shellfish, vegetables, cheese, and even fruit. It is highly nutritious, too, providing slow-burning energy, carbohydrate, and protein. It is also economical, so you can invite friends to dinner more often.

The recipes in this book are mostly designed to serve four people, but quantities can easily be doubled or tripled for larger parties. A specific type of pasta is suggested in each recipe, but you can substitute your own favorites.

Pasta Types

When buying dried pasta, choose good-quality well-known brands. Of the "fresh" pasta sold in sealed packages in super-markets, the filled or stuffed varieties are worth buying; noodles and ribbon pasta are better bought dried, as these tend to have more bite when cooked. However, if you are lucky enough to live near an Italian deli where pasta is made on the premises, it will usually be of very good quality. Fresh is not nec-essarily better, but the final choice is yours – the best pasta is homemade, as you can be sure of the quality of the ingredients used and also of the finished texture.

You will see from this book that the sauces are almost limitless in their variety, as are the pasta shapes themselves. There are no hard-and-fast rules regarding which shape to use with which pasta sauce: it's really a matter of personal preference. However, there are a few guidelines to follow, such as that thin spaghetti suits seafood sauces, thicker spaghetti is good with creamy sauces and thick tubular pasta, like rigatoni, penne and so on, suits rustic sauces full of bits that will be caught in the pasta itself.

macaroni

vermicelli

quick-cook
macaroni

fresh cuttlefish-ink
tagliatelle

tagliatelle: tomato,
spinach and plain

orzo or puntalette

small soup pasta

fresh caramellone

lasagne lunghe

fresh ravioli

fresh cappelletti

fresh paglia e fieno
("straw and hay" tagliarini)

fresh tortellini

fresh pappardelle

fresh beet
tagliatelle

whole wheat spaghetti

tomato spaghetti

spinach spaghetti

pipe rigate

fresh wild-mushroom
tagliatelle

campanelle

conchigliette rigate
(small soup pasta shells)

farfalle (pasta bows)

cannelloni

fettuccia riccia

pasta shells (conchiglie)

spirali

rigatoni

lasagne

spinach lasagne

garganelle

whole wheat shells

orecchiette

Sauces and Pastes

There is an infinite variety of pre-made sauces and pastes available which you can add to your own sauce to make it richer or to deepen the flavor. Some can even be incorporated into pasta dough: for example, you can make mushroom or tomato or even pesto pasta.

Anchovies: salted Whole anchovies preserved in salt need to be rinsed and the backbone removed before use. They have a fresher flavor than canned anchovy fillets in oil. Used in moderation, anchovies add a fishy depth to sauces and soups.

Capers These are little green flower buds preserved in vinegar or salt. They add a sharp piquancy to rich sauces and are especially good with tomatoes and many cheeses.

Carbonara sauce This is a delicious sauce made from cream, eggs, Parmesan and bacon or pancetta. Pre-made carbonara sauce is a useful standby for a quick meal – add sautéed fresh mushrooms or more bacon, if wished.

Garlic: chopped A great time-saver, eliminating the need for peeling and chopping. Use it straight out of the jar.

Mushroom paste A delicacy available from Italian delis. Add a generous spoonful to freshly cooked pasta with a little cream for a quick sauce, or incorporate it into dough to make delicious mushroom pasta.

Olive paste Cuts out all that pitting and chopping. Delicious stirred into hot pasta with chopped fresh tomato, or added by the spoonful to enrich a sauce.

Pesto The commercial version of fresh basil pesto. Brands vary, but it is a very useful pantry standby to stir into hot pasta and soups.

Pesto: fresh Some supermarkets produce their own "fresh" pesto, sold in tubs in the fridge section. This is infinitely superior to the bottled variety, although your own freshly made pesto will be even better.

Pesto: red A commercial sauce made from tomatoes and red bell peppers to stir into hot pasta or to pep up soups.

Tomato pasta sauce Again, a good standby or base for a quick meal. Vary by adding chopped anchovies and olives, or pour over freshly cooked stuffed pasta such as tortellini.

Tomato paste An essential if you are making a sauce from insipid fresh tomatoes. It intensifies any tomato-based sauce and helps thicken meat sauces. It can also be added to the basic dough.

Tomatoes: canned plum No pantry should be without these – invaluable for making any tomato sauce or stew when good, fresh tomatoes are not readily available.

Tomatoes: canned chopped Usually made from Italian plum tomatoes which have a fuller flavor than most, these are the heart of a good tomato sauce if you cannot find really ripe, red, tasty, fresh tomatoes.

Tomatoes: strained A useful pantry ingredient, this is pulped tomato that has been strained to remove the seeds. It makes a good base for a tomato sauce, though chopped canned tomatoes can also be used.

Tomatoes: sun-dried in oil These tomatoes are drained and chopped and added to tomato-based dishes to give a deeper, almost roasted tomato flavor.

Below, clockwise from top left: Salted anchovies; canned chopped tomatoes; pesto; olive paste; canned plum tomatoes; tomato purée; passata.

Eastern Pasta

Various forms of noodle or pasta exist outside Europe and America. They are found mainly in China and Japan, but also throughout Malaysia, Hong Kong and the rest of the Far East, including parts of India and Tibet.

This pasta, usually in noodle form and often enhanced with a sprinkling of vegetables or fish, adds variety to the sometimes monotonous staple diet of rice and beans eaten by the poorer sections of the population. Some types of pasta are used to give bulk to soups; others are eaten as a filling dish to stave off hunger during the day. They are made from the staple crops of each region – whether rice flour, soy bean flour or potato flour – and are cooked in different ways: some are soaked and then fried, some are boiled and fried and some are rolled out and stuffed like ravioli, but most are simply boiled. Some turn transparent when cooked.

Oriental egg noodles are usually made with wheat flour and can be treated in the same way as ordinary Western pasta. Buckwheat and fresh whole wheat noodles are cooked in a similar fashion. Fresh white noodles do not contain egg but are cooked in the same way as egg noodles. Some dried egg noodles come in disks or blocks and are "cooked" by immersion in boiling water in which they are then soaked for a few minutes. As with Western pasta, oriental noodles can be flavored with additional

ingredients such as shrimp, carrot and spinach.

Won ton skins, like thin squares of rolled-out pasta, are used for stuffing and making different filled shapes. Although oriental pasta is available in a variety of long noodle types, it doesn't seem to be made into the shapes we are used to seeing in Europe and America: you will often find it wound into balls and beautifully packaged.

Above: Eastern noodles include (from top left, clockwise) oriental rice flour noodles, rice vermicelli, rice stick noodles, handmade amoy flour vermicelli, medium egg noodles, fresh brown mein, egg noodles, rice stick vermicelli, fresh thin egg noodles, Japanese wheat flour noodles, Ho Fan vermicelli, spinach vegetable noodles, carrot vegetable noodles, won ton skins, wheat flour noodles, fresh white mein, buckwheat noodles, shrimp egg noodles.

About Pasta

Most pasta is made from durum wheat flour and water – durum is a special kind of wheat with a very high protein content. Egg pasta, *pasta all'uova*, contains flour and eggs, and is used for flat pasta such as tagliatelle, or for lasagne. Very little whole wheat pasta is eaten in Italy, but it is quite popular in other countries.

All these types of pasta are available dried in packages and will keep almost indefinitely. Fresh pasta is now widely available and can be bought in most good supermarkets. It can be very good, but can never compare to homemade egg pasta.

Pasta comes in countless shapes and sizes. It is very difficult to give a definitive list, as the names for the shapes vary from country to country. In some cases, just within Italy, the same shape can appear with several different names, depending upon which region it is in. The pasta shapes called for in this book, as well as many others, are illustrated in the introduction. The most common names have been listed there.

Most of the recipes in this book specify the pasta shape most appropriate for a particular sauce. They can, of course, be replaced with another kind. A general rule is that long pasta goes better with tomato or thinner sauces, while short pasta is best for chunkier, meatier sauces. But this rule should not be followed too rigidly. Part of the fun of cooking and eating pasta is in the endless possible combinations of sauce and pasta shapes.

How to Make Egg Pasta by Hand

This classic recipe for egg pasta from Emilia Romagna region, around Bologna, calls for just three ingredients: flour, eggs and a little salt. In other regions of Italy, water, milk or oil are sometimes added. Use all-purpose or white bread flour, and large eggs. As a general guide, use ½ cup of flour to each egg. Quantities will vary with the exact size of the eggs.

To serve 3–4

1¼ cups flour

2 eggs

pinch of salt

To serve 4–6

scant 2 cups flour

3 eggs

pinch of salt

To serve 6–8

2½ cups flour

4 eggs

pinch of salt

1 Place the flour in the center of a clean, smooth work surface. Make a well in the middle. Break the eggs into the well. Add a pinch of salt.

2 Start beating the eggs with a fork, gradually drawing the flour from the inside walls of the well. As the pasta thickens, continue the mixing with your hands. Incorporate as much flour as possible until the mixture forms a mass. It will still be fairly lumpy. If it still sticks to your hands, add a little more flour. Set the dough aside. Using the back of a large knife, scrape off all traces of the dough from the work surface until it is perfectly smooth. Wash and dry your hands. Lightly flour the work surface.

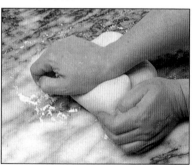

3 Knead the dough by pressing it away from you with the heel of your hands, and then folding it over toward you. Repeat this action over and over, turning the dough as you knead. Work for about 10 minutes, or until the dough is smooth and elastic.

4 If you are using more than two eggs, divide the dough in half. Flour the rolling pin and the work surface. Pat the dough into a disk and begin rolling it out into a flat circle, rotating it a quarter turn after each roll to keep its shape round. Roll until the disk is about ⅛ inch thick.

sheet each time to keep it evenly thin. By the end (this should not last more than 8–10 minutes or the dough will lose its elasticity), the whole sheet should be smooth and almost transparent. If the dough is still sticky, lightly flour your hands as you continue rolling and stretching it in the same way.

8 To cut tagliatelle, fettuccine or tagliolini, fold the sheet of pasta into a flat roll about 4 inches wide. Cut across the roll to form noodles of the desired width. Tagliolini is ⅛ inch; fettuccine is ⅙ inch; tagliatelle is ¼ inch. After cutting, open out the noodles and let them dry for about 5 minutes before cooking. These noodles may be stored for some weeks in the fridge and they can also be frozen successfully. Always allow the noodles to dry completely before storing and use as required.

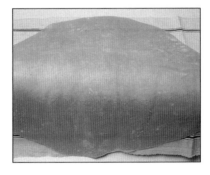

5 Roll out the dough until it is paper-thin by rolling up on to the rolling pin and simultaneously giving a sideways stretch with your hands. Wrap the near edge of the dough around the center of the rolling pin and begin rolling the dough up away from you. As you roll back and forth, slide your hands from the center toward the outer edges of the pin, stretching and thinning out the pasta.

6 Quickly repeat these movements until about two-thirds of the sheet of pasta is wrapped around the pin. Lift and turn the wrapped pasta sheet about 45° before unrolling it. Repeat the rolling and stretching process, starting from a new point of the

7 If you are making pasta noodles, such as tagliatelle or fettuccine, lay a clean dish towel on a table or other flat surface, and unroll the pasta sheet onto it, letting about a third of the sheet hang over the edge of the table. Rotate the dough about every 10 minutes. Roll out the second sheet of dough if you are using more than two eggs. After 25–30 minutes the pasta will have dried enough to cut. Do not let it over-dry or the pasta will crack as it is cut.

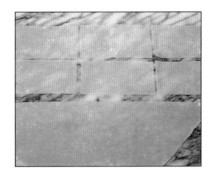

9 To cut the pasta for lasagne or pappardelle, do not fold or dry the rolled-out dough. Lasagne is made from rectangles of about 5 × 3½ inches. Pappardelle are large noodles cut with a fluted pasta or pastry wheel. They are about ¾ inches wide.

SOUPS

Provençal Fish Soup with Pasta

This colorful soup has all the flavors of the Mediterranean. Serve it as a main course for a deliciously filling lunch.

INGREDIENTS

Serves 4

2 tablespoons olive oil

1 onion, sliced

1 garlic clove, crushed

1 leek, sliced

8 ounces canned chopped tomatoes

pinch of Mediterranean herbs

¼ teaspoon saffron strands (optional)

4 ounces small pasta

about 8 live mussels in the shell

1 pound filleted and skinned white fish,
    such as cod, sand dab or monkfish

salt and ground black pepper

For the rouille

2 garlic cloves, crushed

1 canned pimiento, drained and chopped

1 tablespoon fresh white bread crumbs

4 tablespoons mayonnaise

toasted French bread, to serve

1 Heat the oil in a large saucepan and add the onion, garlic and leek. Cover and cook gently for 5 minutes, stirring occasionally until the vegetables are soft.

2 Pour in 4 cups water, the tomatoes, herbs, saffron and pasta. Season with salt and ground black pepper and cook for 15–20 minutes.

3 Scrub the mussels and pull off the "beards." Discard any that will not close when sharply tapped.

4 Cut the fish into bite-size chunks and add to the soup, placing the mussels on top. Then simmer with the lid on for 5–10 minutes until the mussels open and the fish is just cooked. Discard any unopened mussels.

5 To make the rouille, pound the garlic, canned pimiento and bread crumbs together in a mortar and pestle (or in a blender or food processor). Stir in the mayonnaise and season well.

6 Spread the toasted French bread with the rouille and serve with the soup.

Pasta, Bean and Vegetable Soup

This colorful, filling soup will satisfy the largest appetite.

INGREDIENTS

Serves 4–6

¾ cup dried borlotti or black-eyed peas, soaked overnight and drained

5 cups vegetable, poultry or meat stock

1 large onion, chopped

1 large garlic clove, finely chopped

2 celery stalks, chopped

½ red bell pepper, seeded and chopped

4 small tomatoes, skinned, seeded and chopped or canned chopped tomatoes

8 thick slices smoked bacon loin

3 ounces tiny soup pasta

2 zucchini, halved lengthwise and sliced

1 tablespoon tomato paste

salt and ground black pepper

shredded fresh basil, to garnish

1 Put the beans in a large pan. Cover with fresh cold water and bring to a boil. Boil for 10 minutes, then drain and rinse. Return the beans to the pan, add the stock and bring to a boil. Skim off the scum.

2 Add the onion, garlic, celery, red pepper, tomatoes and bacon. Bring back to a boil.

3 Cover and simmer over low heat for about 1½ hours, or until the beans are just tender. Lift out the bacon. Shred the meat with two forks and set aside.

4 Add the pasta, zucchini and tomato paste to the soup. Season to taste with salt and freshly ground pepper. Simmer, uncovered, for 5–8 minutes more, stirring the soup occasionally. (Check the pasta cooking time on the package.)

5 Stir in the shredded bacon. Taste and adjust the seasoning if necessary, then serve the soup hot, sprinkled with shredded fresh basil as a garnish.

Zucchini Soup with Small Pasta Shells

A pretty, fresh-tasting soup which could be made using cucumber instead of zucchini.

INGREDIENTS

Serves 4–6

4 tablespoons olive or sunflower oil

2 onions, finely chopped

6¼ cups chicken stock

2 pounds zucchini

4 ounces small soup pasta

freshly squeezed lemon juice

2 tablespoons chopped fresh chervil

salt and ground black pepper

sour cream, to serve

1 Heat the oil in a large saucepan and add the onions. Cover and cook gently for about 20 minutes until very soft but not colored, stirring occasionally.

2 Add the chicken stock to the saucepan and bring the mixture to a boil.

3 Meanwhile, grate the zucchini and stir into the boiling stock with the pasta. Reduce the heat and simmer for 15 minutes until the pasta is tender. Season to taste with lemon juice, salt and pepper.

4 Stir in the chopped fresh chervil and add a swirl of sour cream before serving.

Chunky Pasta Soup

Serve this filling main-meal soup with tasty, pesto-topped French bread croûtons.

INGREDIENTS

Serves 4

⅔ cup dry beans (a mixture of red kidney and haricot beans), soaked in cold water overnight

1 tablespoon oil

1 onion, chopped

2 celery stalks, thinly sliced

2–3 garlic cloves, crushed

2 leeks, thinly sliced

1 vegetable stock cube

14-ounce can or jar of pimientos

3–4 tablespoons tomato paste

4 ounces pasta shapes

4 pieces French bread

1 tablespoon pesto sauce

1 cup baby corn, halved

2 ounces each broccoli and cauliflower florets

few drops of Tabasco sauce, to taste

salt and ground black pepper

1 Drain the beans and place in a large saucepan with 5 cups water. Bring to a boil and simmer for about 1 hour, or until the beans are nearly tender.

2 When the beans are almost ready, heat the oil in a large pan and fry the vegetables for 2 minutes. Add the stock cube and the beans with 2 cups of their liquid. Cover and simmer for about 10 minutes.

3 Meanwhile, liquidize the pimientos with a little of their liquid and add to the pan. Stir in the tomato paste and pasta and cook for 15 minutes. Preheat the oven to 400°F.

4 Meanwhile, make the pesto croûtons: spread the French bread with the pesto sauce and bake for 10 minutes, or until crispy.

5 When the pasta is just cooked, add the corn, broccoli and cauliflower florets, Tabasco sauce and seasoning to taste. Heat through for 2–3 minutes and serve immediately with the croûtons.

Red Onion and Beet Soup

This beautiful, vivid ruby-red soup will look stunning at any dinner-party table.

Serves 4–6

1 tablespoon olive oil

2 red onions, sliced

2 garlic cloves, crushed

10 ounces cooked beets, cut into sticks

5 cups vegetable stock or water

2 ounces cooked soup pasta

2 tablespoons raspberry vinegar

salt and ground black pepper

low-fat yogurt or fromage blanc,
   to garnish

chopped chives, to garnish

3 Add the beets, stock or water, cooked soup pasta and vinegar, and heat through. Season to taste with salt and pepper.

4 Ladle into soup bowls. Top each one with a spoonful of low-fat yogurt or fromage blanc and sprinkle with chives.

1 Heat the olive oil in a flame-proof casserole and add the onions and garlic.

2 Cook gently for 20 minutes, or until the onions and garlic are soft and tender.

Thai Chicken Soup

This classic Asian soup now enjoys worldwide popularity.

INGREDIENTS

Serves 4

1 tablespoon vegetable oil

1 garlic clove, finely chopped

2 boneless chicken breasts, about 6 ounces each, skinned and chopped

½ teaspoon ground turmeric

¼ teaspoon hot chili powder

3 ounces creamed coconut

3¾ cups hot chicken stock

2 tablespoons lemon or lime juice

2 tablespoons crunchy peanut butter

2 ounces thread egg noodles, broken into small pieces

1 tablespoon scallions, finely chopped

1 tablespoon chopped fresh cilantro

salt and ground black pepper

2 tablespoons dried coconut and ½ fresh red chili, seeded and finely chopped, to garnish

1 Heat the oil in a large pan and fry the garlic for 1 minute until lightly golden. Add the chicken and spices and stir-fry 3–4 minutes more.

2 Crumble the creamed coconut into the hot chicken stock and stir until dissolved. Pour onto the chicken, then add the lemon or lime juice, peanut butter and egg noodles.

3 Cover and simmer for about 15 minutes. Add the scallions and fresh cilantro, then season well and cook for 5 minutes more.

4 Meanwhile, place the coconut and chili in a small frying pan and heat for 2–3 minutes, stirring frequently, until the coconut is lightly browned.

5 Serve the soup in warmed bowls sprinkled with the fried coconut and chili.

Parmesan and Cauliflower Soup

A silky-smooth, mildly cheesy soup which isn't overpowered by the cauliflower. It makes an elegant dinner-party soup served with crisp Melba toast.

Serves 6

1 large cauliflower
5 cups chicken or vegetable stock
6 ounces farfalle
⅔ cup light cream or milk
freshly grated nutmeg
pinch of cayenne pepper
4 tablespoons freshly grated
    Parmesan cheese
salt and ground black pepper

For the Melba toast
3–4 slices day-old white bread
freshly grated Parmesan cheese,
    for sprinkling
¼ teaspoon paprika

3 Add the pasta to the stock and simmer for 10 minutes until tender. Drain, reserve the pasta, and pour the liquid over the cauliflower. Add the cream or milk, nutmeg and cayenne to the cauliflower. Blend until smooth, then press through a strainer. Stir in the cooked pasta. Reheat the soup and stir in the Parmesan. Taste and adjust the seasoning, if necessary.

4 Meanwhile, make the Melba toast. Preheat the oven to 350°F. Toast the bread lightly on both sides. Quickly cut off the crusts and split each slice in half horizontally. Scrape off any doughy bits and sprinkle with Parmesan and paprika. Place on a baking sheet and bake in the oven for about 10–15 minutes, or until uniformly golden. Serve with the hot soup.

1 Cut the leaves and central stalk away from the cauliflower and discard. Divide the cauliflower into similar-size florets.

2 Bring the stock to a boil and add the cauliflower. Simmer for about 10 minutes, or until very soft. Remove the cauliflower with a slotted spoon and place in a blender or food processor.

Minestrone

A substantial and popular winter soup originally from Milan, but found in various versions around the Mediterranean coasts of Italy and France. Cut the vegetables as coarsely or as small as you like. Add freshly grated Parmesan cheese just before serving.

INGREDIENTS

Serves 6–8

2 cups dried haricot beans
2 tablespoons olive oil
⅓ cup smoked lean bacon, diced
2 large onions, sliced
2 garlic cloves, crushed
2 carrots, diced
3 celery stalks, sliced
14-ounce can chopped tomatoes
10 cups beef stock
12 ounces potatoes, diced
6 ounces small pasta shapes, such as
    macaroni, stars, shells
2 cups green cabbage, thinly sliced
1½ cups fine green beans, sliced
1 cup frozen peas
3 tablespoons chopped fresh parsley
salt and ground black pepper
freshly grated Parmesan cheese, to serve

1 Cover the beans with cold water in a bowl and let them soak overnight.

2 Heat the oil in a large saucepan and add the bacon, onions and garlic. Cover and cook gently for 5 minutes, stirring occasionally.

3 Add the carrots and celery and cook for 2–3 minutes until the vegetables are softening.

4 Drain the beans and add to the saucepan with the tomatoes and the beef stock. Cover and simmer for 2–2½ hours, or until the beans are tender.

5 Add the potatoes 30 minutes before the soup is ready.

6 Add the pasta, cabbage, green beans, peas and parsley at least 15 minutes before the soup is ready. Season to taste and serve with a bowl of freshly grated Parmesan cheese.

Consommé with Agnolotti

A delicious and satisfying consommé with wonderful flavors.

Serves 4–6

3 ounces cooked peeled shrimp

3 ounces canned crabmeat, drained

1 teaspoon fresh ginger, peeled and
   finely grated

1 tablespoon fresh white bread crumbs

1 teaspoon light soy sauce

1 scallion, finely chopped

1 garlic clove, crushed

1 quantity of basic pasta dough

flour, for dusting

egg white, beaten

14-ounce can chicken or fish consommé

2 tablespoons sherry or vermouth

salt and ground black pepper

2 ounces cooked peeled shrimp and fresh
   cilantro leaves, to garnish

1 To make the filling, put the shrimp, crabmeat, ginger, bread crumbs, soy sauce, scallion, garlic and seasoning into a food processor or blender and process until smooth.

2 Roll the pasta into thin sheets and dust lightly with flour. Stamp out 32 rounds about 2 inches in diameter, with a fluted pastry cutter.

3 Place a small teaspoon of the filling in the center of half the pasta rounds. Brush the edges of each round with egg white and sandwich together with a second round on top. Pinch the edges together firmly to stop the filling seeping out.

4 Cook the pasta in a large pan of boiling, salted water for 5 minutes (cook in batches to stop them sticking together). Remove and drop into a bowl of cold water for 5 seconds before placing on a tray. (You can make these pasta shapes a day in advance. Cover with plastic wrap and store in the fridge until required.)

5 Heat the chicken or fish consommé in a pan with the sherry or vermouth. When piping hot, add the pasta shapes and simmer for 1–2 minutes.

6 Serve pasta in a shallow soup bowl covered with hot consommé. Garnish with extra peeled shrimp and fresh cilantro.

F I S H &
S H E L L F I S H
D I S H E S

Tuna Lasagne

INGREDIENTS

Serves 6

1 quantity fresh pasta dough, cut for
   lasagne, or 12 ounces no-precook
   dried lasagne
1 tablespoon butter
1 small onion, finely chopped
1 garlic clove, finely chopped
1½ cups mushrooms, thinly sliced
4 tablespoons dry white wine (optional)
2½ cups white sauce
⅔ cup whipping cream
3 tablespoons chopped parsley
2 x 7-ounce cans tuna, drained
2 canned pimientos, cut into strips
generous ½ cup frozen peas, thawed
4 ounces mozzarella cheese, grated
2 tablespoons freshly grated
   Parmesan cheese
salt and ground black pepper

1 For fresh lasagne, bring a large pan of salted water to a boil. Cook the lasagne, in small batches, until almost tender to the bite. For dried lasagne, soak in a bowl of hot water for 3–5 minutes.

2 Place the lasagne in a colander and rinse with cold water. Lay on a dish towel to drain.

3 Preheat the oven to 350°F. Melt the butter in a saucepan and cook the onion until soft.

4 Add the garlic and mushrooms, and cook until soft, stirring occasionally. Pour in the wine, if using. Boil for 1 minute. Add the white sauce, cream and parsley. Season.

5 Spoon a layer of sauce over the bottom of a 12 × 9-inch baking dish. Cover with a layer of lasagne sheets.

6 Flake the tuna. Sprinkle half the tuna, pimiento strips, peas and mozzarella over the lasagne. Spoon a third of the remaining sauce over the top and cover with another layer of lasagne sheets.

7 Repeat the layers, ending with pasta and sauce. Sprinkle with the Parmesan. Bake for 30–40 minutes, or until lightly browned.

Pasta Bows with Smoked Salmon and Dill

In Italy, pasta cooked with smoked salmon is very fashionable. This is a quick and luxurious sauce.

INGREDIENTS

Serves 4

6 scallions

4 tablespoons butter

6 tablespoons dry white wine or vermouth

1¾ cups heavy cream

freshly grated nutmeg

8 ounces smoked salmon

2 tablespoons chopped fresh dill, or
    1 tablespoon dried

freshly squeezed lemon juice

1 pound farfalle

salt and ground black pepper

1 Slice the scallions finely. Melt the butter in a saucepan and gently fry the scallions for 1 minute until softened.

2 Add the wine or vermouth and boil hard to reduce to about 2 tablespoons. Stir in the cream and add salt, pepper and nutmeg to taste. Bring to a boil and simmer for 2–3 minutes until the sauce is slightly thickened.

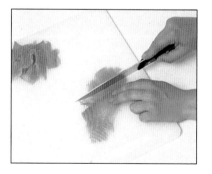

3 Cut the smoked salmon into 1-inch squares and stir into the sauce with the dill. Taste and add a little lemon juice. Keep the sauce warm.

4 Cook the pasta in plenty of boiling salted water according to the instructions on the package. Drain well. Toss the pasta with the sauce and serve immediately.

Spaghetti with Hot-and-sour Fish

A truly Chinese spicy taste is what makes this sauce so different.

INGREDIENTS

Serves 4

12 ounces spaghetti

1 pound monkfish, skinned

8 ounces zucchini

1 green chili, cored and seeded (optional)

1 tablespoon olive oil

1 large onion, chopped

1 teaspoon turmeric

1 cup shelled peas, thawed if frozen

2 teaspoons lemon juice

5 tablespoons hoisin sauce

⅔ cup water

salt and ground black pepper

fresh dill sprig, to garnish

1 Cook the pasta in plenty of boiling salted water according to the instructions on the package.

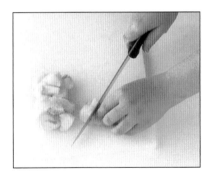

2 Cut the monkfish into bite-size pieces. Thinly slice the zucchini, then finely chop the chili, if using.

3 Heat the oil in a large frying pan and fry the onion for 5 minutes until softened. Add the turmeric.

4 Add the chili, if using, zucchini and peas, and fry over medium heat for 5 minutes until the vegetables have softened.

5 Stir in the fish, lemon juice, hoisin sauce and water. Bring to a boil, then simmer, uncovered, for about 5 minutes or until the fish is tender. Season.

6 Drain the pasta thoroughly and turn into a serving dish. Toss in the sauce to coat. Serve immediately, garnished with fresh dill.

Smoked Trout Cannelloni

Smoked trout can be bought already filleted or whole. If you buy fillets, you'll need 8 ounces.

INGREDIENTS

Serves 4–6

1 large onion, finely chopped

1 garlic clove, crushed

4 tablespoons vegetable stock

2 x 14-ounce cans chopped tomatoes

½ teaspoon dried mixed herbs

1 smoked trout, about 14 ounces

¾ cup frozen peas, thawed

1½ cups fresh bread crumbs

16 cannelloni tubes

salt and ground black pepper

mixed salad, to serve (optional)

1½ tablespoons freshly grated
   Parmesan cheese

For the cheese sauce

2 tablespoons margarine

¼ cup all-purpose flour

1½ cups skim milk

freshly grated nutmeg

1 Simmer the onion, garlic and stock in a large covered saucepan for 3 minutes. Uncover and continue to cook, stirring occasionally, until the stock has reduced entirely.

2 Stir in the tomatoes and dried herbs. Simmer, uncovered, for 10 minutes more, or until the mixture is very thick.

3 Meanwhile, skin the smoked trout with a sharp knife. Carefully flake the flesh and discard the bones. Mix the fish together with the tomato mixture, peas, bread crumbs, salt and ground black pepper.

4 Preheat the oven to 375°F. Spoon the trout filling into the cannelloni tubes and arrange them in a casserole.

5 For the sauce, put the margarine, flour and milk into a saucepan and cook over medium heat, whisking constantly until the sauce thickens. Simmer gently for 2–3 minutes, stirring all the time. Season to taste with salt, ground pepper and nutmeg.

6 Pour the sauce over the cannelloni tubes and sprinkle with the grated Parmesan cheese. Bake in the oven for 35–40 minutes, or until the top is golden and bubbling. Serve with a mixed salad, if liked.

Stir-fried Noodles with Sweet Salmon

A delicious sauce forms the marinade for the salmon in this recipe. Served with soft-fried noodles, it makes a stunning dish.

INGREDIENTS

Serves 4

12 ounces salmon fillet

2 tablespoons Japanese soy sauce (shoyu)

2 tablespoons sake

¼ cup mirin or sweet sherry

1 teaspoon light brown sugar

2 teaspoons grated fresh ginger

3 cloves garlic, 1 crushed, and 2 sliced

2 tablespoons peanut oil

8 ounces dried egg noodles, cooked and drained

2 ounces alfalfa sprouts

2 tablespoons sesame seeds, lightly toasted

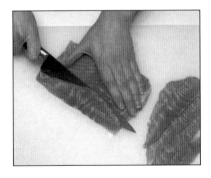

1 Thinly slice the salmon, then place in a shallow dish.

2 In a bowl, combine the soy sauce, sake, mirin, sugar, ginger and crushed garlic. Pour the sauce over the salmon, cover and let marinate for 30 minutes.

3 Drain the salmon, scraping off and reserving the marinade. Place the salmon in a single layer on a baking sheet. Cook under a preheated broiler for 2–3 minutes, without turning.

4 Meanwhile, heat a wok until hot, add the oil and swirl it around. Add the garlic rounds and cook until golden brown, but do not let them burn.

5 Add the cooked noodles and reserved marinade to the wok. Stir-fry for 3–4 minutes, until the marinade has reduced slightly to make a syrupy glaze that coats the egg noodles.

6 Toss in the alfalfa sprouts, then remove immediately from the heat. Transfer to warmed serving plates and top with the salmon. Sprinkle on the toasted sesame seeds. Serve immediately.

COOK'S TIP

It is important to scrape the marinade off the fish, as any remaining pieces of ginger or garlic would burn during grilling and spoil the finished dish.

Pasta with Tuna, Capers and Anchovies

This piquant sauce could be made without the addition of tomatoes – just heat the oil, add the other ingredients and heat through gently before tossing with the pasta.

INGREDIENTS

Serves 4

14-ounce can tunafish in oil
2 tablespoons olive oil
2 garlic cloves, crushed
1¾ pounds canned chopped tomatoes
6 canned anchovy fillets, drained
2 tablespoons capers in vinegar, drained
2 tablespoons chopped fresh basil
1 pound rigatoni, penne or garganelle
salt and ground black pepper
fresh basil sprigs, to garnish

1 Drain the oil from the can of tunafish into a large saucepan, add the olive oil and heat gently until the oil mixture stops spitting.

2 Add the garlic and fry until golden. Stir in the tomatoes and simmer for about 25 minutes until thickened.

3 Flake the tuna and cut the anchovies in half. Stir into the sauce with the capers and chopped basil. Season well.

4 Cook the pasta in plenty of boiling salted water according to the instructions on the package. Drain well and toss with the sauce. Garnish with fresh basil sprigs.

Smoked Haddock and Pasta in Parsley Sauce

A creamy and delicious pasta dish with a crunchy almond topping.

Serves 4

1 pound smoked haddock fillet

1 small leek or onion, sliced thickly

1¼ cups milk

1 bouquet garni (bay leaf, thyme and parsley stalks)

2 tablespoons margarine

2 tablespoons flour

8 ounces pasta shells

2 tablespoons chopped fresh parsley

salt and freshly ground black pepper

½ cup toasted sliced almonds, to garnish

3 Put the margarine, flour and reserved milk into a pan. Bring to a boil and whisk constantly until smooth. Season, then add the fish and leek.

4 Cook the pasta in a large pan of boiling water until tender, but still firm to the bite. Drain and stir into the sauce with the chopped parsley. Serve immediately, scattered with almonds.

1 Remove all the skin and any bones from the haddock. Put into a pan with the leek, milk and bouquet garni. Bring to a boil, cover and simmer gently for 8–10 minutes, until the fish flakes easily.

2 Strain, reserving the milk for making the sauce, and discard the bouquet garni.

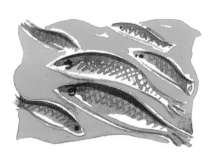

Baked Seafood Spaghetti

In this dish, each portion is baked and served in an individual package which is then opened at the table. Use parchment paper or foil to make the packages.

Serves 4

1 pound fresh mussels

½ cup dry white wine

4 tablespoons olive oil

2 garlic cloves, finely chopped

1 pound tomatoes, fresh or canned, peeled and finely chopped

14 ounces spaghetti or other long pasta

2 cups shelled and deveined shrimp, fresh or frozen

2 tablespoons chopped fresh parsley

salt and ground black pepper

1 Scrub the mussels well under cold running water, cutting off the "beards" with a small, sharp knife. Discard any that do not close when tapped sharply. Place the mussels and the wine in a large saucepan and heat until opened.

2 Lift out the mussels and remove to a side dish. Discard any that do not open. Strain the cooking liquid into a bowl through paper towels and reserve until needed. Preheat the oven to 300°F.

3 In a medium saucepan, heat the oil and garlic together for 1–2 minutes. Add the tomatoes and cook over moderate to high heat until softened. Stir ¾ cup of the mussel cooking liquid into the saucepan.

4 Cook the pasta in plenty of boiling salted water until *al dente*. Just before draining the pasta, add the shrimp and parsley to the tomato sauce. Cook for 2 minutes. Taste for seasoning, adding salt and pepper, if necessary. Remove from the heat.

5 Prepare four pieces of parchment paper or foil about 12 × 18 inches. Place each sheet in the center of a shallow bowl. Turn the drained pasta into a mixing bowl. Add the tomato sauce and mix well. Stir in the mussels.

6 Divide the pasta and seafood among the four pieces of paper or foil, placing a mound in the center of each, and twisting the ends together to make a closed package. Arrange on a large baking sheet and place in the center of the oven. Bake for 8–10 minutes. Place the unopened packages on individual serving plates.

Tagliatelle with Smoked Salmon

This is a pretty pasta dish with the light texture of the cucumber complementing the fish perfectly.

INGREDIENTS

Serves 4

12 ounces tagliatelle

½ cucumber

6 tablespoons butter

grated rind of 1 orange

2 tablespoons chopped fresh dill

1¼ cups light cream

1 tablespoon orange juice

4 ounces smoked salmon, skinned

salt and ground black pepper

1 Cook the pasta in plenty of boiling salted water according to the instructions on the package.

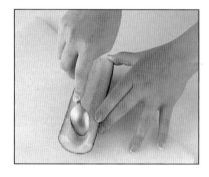

2 Using a sharp knife, cut the cucumber in half lengthwise then, using a small spoon, scoop out the seeds and discard.

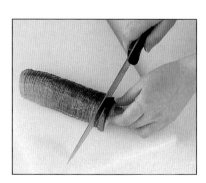

3 Turn the cucumber on the flat side and slice thinly.

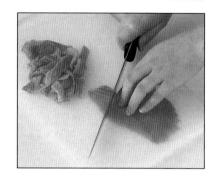

4 Melt the butter in a saucepan, add the orange rind and dill and stir well. Add the cucumber and cook gently for 2 minutes, stirring occasionally.

5 Add the cream and orange juice, and season to taste. Then simmer for 1 minute.

6 Meanwhile, cut the salmon into thin strips. Stir into the sauce and heat through.

7 Drain the pasta thoroughly and toss in the sauce until well coated. Serve immediately.

Spaghetti with Clams

Try chopped fresh dill for a delicious alternative in this dish.

INGREDIENTS

Serves 4

24 live clams in the shell, scrubbed

1 cup water

½ cup dry white wine

1 pound spaghetti, preferably Italian

5 tablespoons olive oil

2 garlic cloves, ground

3 tablespoons chopped fresh parsley

salt and ground black pepper

1 Rinse the clams well in cold water and drain. Place in a large saucepan with the water and wine and bring to a boil. Cover and steam until the shells open, about 6–8 minutes.

2 Discard any clams that have not opened. Remove the clams from their shells. If large, chop them coarsely.

3 Strain the cooking liquid through a strainer lined with muslin. Place in a small saucepan and boil rapidly until reduced by about half. Set aside.

4 Cook the spaghetti in plenty of boiling salted water, according to the instructions on the package, until *al dente.*

5 Meanwhile, heat the olive oil in a large frying pan. Add the garlic and cook for 2–3 minutes, but do not let it brown. Add the reduced clam liquid and the parsley. Cook over low heat until the spaghetti is ready.

6 Drain the spaghetti. Add to the frying pan, increase the heat to medium, and add the clams. Cook for 3–4 minutes, stirring, to coat the spaghetti with the sauce and to heat the clams.

7 Season with salt and pepper and serve immediately.

Pasta with Shrimp and Feta Cheese

This dish combines the richness of fresh shrimp with the tartness of feta cheese. Goat cheese could also be used, if preferred.

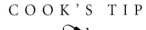

INGREDIENTS

Serves 4

1 pound raw shrimp in the shell

6 scallions

8 ounces feta cheese

4 tablespoons butter

small bunch fresh chives

1 pound penne, garganelle or rigatoni

salt and ground black pepper

COOK'S TIP

~

If fresh shrimp are not available, use well-thawed frozen, and add to the sauce at the last minute together with the scallions.

1 Remove the heads from the shrimp by twisting and pulling them off. Shell the shrimp and discard the shells.

2 On a nylon chopping board, chop the scallions and cut the feta cheese into 1/2-inch cubes.

3 Melt the butter in a frying pan and stir in the shrimp. When they turn pink, add the scallions and cook gently over low heat for about 1 minute.

4 Stir the feta cheese into the shrimp mixture. Season with black pepper.

5 Cut the chives into 1-inch lengths and stir half into the shrimp mixture.

6 Cook the pasta in plenty of boiling salted water according to the instructions on the package. Drain well, pile into a warmed serving dish and top with the sauce. Sprinkle with the remaining chives and serve.

Fried Singapore Noodles

Thai fishcakes vary in their size and their spiciness. They are available from Asian supermarkets.

Serves 4

6 ounces rice noodles

4 tablespoons vegetable oil

½ teaspoon salt

¾ cup cooked shrimp

6 ounces cooked pork, cut
    into matchsticks

1 green bell pepper, seeded and cut
    into matchsticks

½ teaspoon sugar

2 teaspoons curry powder

3 ounces Thai fishcakes

2 teaspoons dark soy sauce

1 Soak the rice noodles in water for about 10 minutes, drain well through a colander, then pat dry with paper towels.

2 Heat a wok, then add half the oil. When the oil is hot, add the noodles and some salt and stir-fry for 2 minutes. Transfer to a warmed serving dish and keep warm.

3 Heat the remaining oil and add the shrimp, pork, bell pepper, sugar, curry powder and remaining salt. Stir-fry for 1 minute.

4 Return the noodles to the pan and stir-fry with the Thai fishcakes for 2 minutes. Stir in the soy sauce and serve immediately.

Shrimp with Tagliatelle in Packages

A quick and impressive dish, easy to prepare in advance and cook at the last minute. When the paper packages are opened at the table, the filling smells wonderful.

INGREDIENTS

Serves 4

1¾ pounds raw shrimp in the shell

1 pound tagliatelle or similar pasta

⅔ cup fresh or pre-made pesto sauce

4 teaspoons olive oil

1 garlic clove, crushed

½ cup dry white wine

salt and ground black pepper

1 Preheat the oven to 400°F. Twist the heads off the shrimp and discard.

2 Cook the tagliatelle in plenty of rapidly boiling salted water for 2 minutes only, then drain. Mix with half the pesto.

3 Cut four 12-inch squares of wax paper and place 1 teaspoon olive oil in the center of each. Pile equal amounts of pasta in the middle of each square.

4 Top with equal amounts of shrimp and spoon on the remaining pesto mixed with the garlic. Season with pepper and sprinkle each with the wine.

5 Brush the edges of the paper lightly with water and bring them loosely up around the filling, twisting to enclose. (The packages should look like money bags.)

6 Place the packages on a baking sheet. Bake in the oven for 10–15 minutes. Serve immediately, allowing the diners to open their own packages at the table.

Saffron Pappardelle

A wonderful dish with a delicious shellfish sauce.

Serves 4

large pinch saffron strands
4 sun-dried tomatoes, chopped
1 teaspoon fresh thyme
12 large shrimp in their shells
8 ounce baby squid
8 ounce monkfish fillet
2–3 garlic cloves
2 small onions, quartered
1 small fennel bulb, trimmed and sliced
²⁄₃ cup white wine
8 ounces pappardelle
salt and ground black pepper
2 tablespoons chopped fresh parsley,
   to garnish

1 Put the saffron, sun-dried tomatoes and thyme into a bowl with 4 tablespoons hot water. Let soak for 30 minutes.

2 Wash the shrimp and carefully remove the shells, leaving the heads and tails intact. Pull the body from the squid and remove the quill. Cut the tentacles from the head and rinse under cold water. Pull off the outer skin and cut into ¼-inch rings. Cut the monkfish into 1-inch cubes.

3 Put the garlic, onions and fennel into a pan with the wine. Cover and simmer for 5 minutes until tender.

4 Add the monkfish, and the saffron, tomatoes and thyme in their liquid. Cover and cook for 3 minutes. Then add the shrimp and squid. Cover and cook gently for 1–2 minutes (do not overcook or the squid will become tough).

5 Meanwhile, cook the pasta in a large pan of boiling, salted water until *al dente*. Drain well.

6 Divide the pasta among four serving dishes and top with the fish and shellfish sauce. Sprinkle with parsley and serve at once.

Black Pasta with Scallops

A stunning pasta dish using black tagliatelle.

INGREDIENTS

Serves 4

½ cup low-fat crème fraîche

2 teaspoons whole-grain mustard

2 garlic cloves, crushed

2–3 tablespoons fresh lime juice

4 tablespoons chopped fresh parsley

2 tablespoons chopped chives

12 ounces black tagliatelle

12 large scallops

4 tablespoons white wine

⅔ cup fish stock

salt and ground black pepper

lime wedges and parsley sprigs, to garnish

1 To make the tartare sauce, combine the crème fraîche, mustard, garlic, lime juice, herbs and seasoning in a bowl.

2 Cook the pasta in a large pan of boiling, salted water until *al dente*. Drain thoroughly.

3 Slice the scallops in half horizontally. Keep any coral whole. Put the white wine and fish stock into a saucepan and heat to simmering point. Add the scallops and cook gently for 3–4 minutes (do not overcook or they will become tough).

4 Remove the scallops. Boil the wine and stock to reduce by half and add the green sauce to the pan. Heat gently to warm, replace the scallops and cook gently for 1 minute. Spoon over the pasta and garnish with lime wedges and sprigs of parsley.

MEAT &
POULTRY
DISHES

Rotolo di Pasta

A giant jelly roll of pasta with a spinach filling, which is poached, sliced and baked with béchamel or tomato sauce. Use fresh homemade pasta for this recipe, or ask your local Italian deli to make a large sheet of pasta for you!

INGREDIENTS

Serves 6

1½ pounds frozen chopped
    spinach, thawed

4 tablespoons butter

1 onion, chopped

4 ounces ham or bacon, diced

8 ounces ricotta or curd cheese

1 egg

freshly grated nutmeg

fresh spinach pasta made with 2 eggs and
    1¾ cups flour

5 cups béchamel sauce, warmed

½ cup freshly grated Parmesan cheese

salt and ground black pepper

3 Roll the fresh pasta out to a rectangle about 12 × 16 inches. Spread the filling all over, leaving a ½-inch border all around the edge of the rectangle.

4 Roll up from the shorter end and wrap in muslin to form a "sausage," tying the ends securely with string. Poach in a very large pan (or fish kettle) of simmering water for 20 minutes, or until firm. Carefully remove, drain and then unwrap. Let cool.

5 When you are ready to finish the dish, preheat the oven to 400°F. Cut the pasta roll into 1-inch slices. Spoon a little béchamel sauce over the bottom of a shallow casserole and arrange the slices on top, slightly overlapping each other.

6 Spoon on the remaining sauce, sprinkle with the Parmesan cheese and bake for 15–20 minutes or until browned and bubbling. Let stand for a few minutes before serving.

1 Squeeze the excess moisture from the spinach and set aside.

2 Melt the butter in a saucepan and fry the onion until golden. Add the ham and fry until beginning to brown. Take off the heat and stir in the spinach. Let cool slightly, then beat in the cheese and the egg. Season with salt, pepper and nutmeg.

Macaroni with Ham and Tomato Sauce

This delicious dish can be cooked in moments and is absolutely perfect for entertaining unexpected guests.

INGREDIENTS

Serves 4

12 ounces dried short-cut macaroni

3 tablespoons olive oil

1 beefsteak tomato, chopped

1 clove garlic, chopped

6 ounces cooked ham, cut into thick strips

6 ounces goat cheese, diced

3 tablespoons fresh oregano leaves

salt and freshly ground black pepper

diced goat cheese and oregano leaves,
   to garnish

1 Cook the pasta in a large pan of lightly salted, boiling water for 8–10 minutes, until tender but still firm to the bite.

2 Meanwhile, heat the oil in a large skillet. Add the tomato, garlic and ham and sauté for 3 minutes.

> ### COOK'S TIP
> ∽
> Goat cheese is available in many forms, such as in herbed oil, coated with coarsely ground pepper, and plain.

3 Lower the heat slightly, stir in the goat cheese and oregano and simmer for a further 30 seconds. Season to taste with salt and pepper.

4 Drain the pasta thoroughly and toss with the sauce. Transfer to a warm serving dish and serve immediately, garnished with diced goat cheese and oregano leaves.

Orechiette with Pork in Mustard Sauce

This country-style dish would taste even better made with wild mushrooms, such as ceps.

INGREDIENTS

Serves 4

12 ounces dried orechiette

4 tablespoons olive oil

2 cloves garlic, chopped

12 ounces pork tenderloin,
   thinly sliced

4 tablespoons butter

6 ounces open-cap mushrooms, sliced

1 tablespoon wholegrain mustard

3 tablespoons snipped fresh chives

salt and freshly ground black pepper

snipped fresh chives, to garnish

1 Cook the pasta in a large saucepan of lightly salted, boiling water for approximately 8–10 minutes, until tender, but still firm to the bite.

2 Meanwhile, heat the oil in a large skillet. Add the garlic and pork and fry, stirring occasionally, for 10 minutes, until the pork is browned and tender.

3 Add the butter, mushrooms and mustard and cook, stirring occasionally, for 2 minutes. Add the chives and season to taste with salt and pepper.

4 Meanwhile, drain the pasta thoroughly. Stir it into the pork mixture and cook for 1 minute, until heated through. Transfer to a warm serving dish, garnish with snipped fresh chives, and serve immediately.

Tagliatelle with Prosciutto and Parmesan

This is a really simple dish, prepared in minutes from the best ingredients.

Serves 4

4 ounces prosciutto

1 pound tagliatelle

6 tablespoons butter

½ cup freshly grated Parmesan cheese

salt and ground black pepper

a few fresh sage leaves, to garnish

1 Cut the prosciutto into strips the same width as the tagliatelle. Cook the pasta in plenty of boiling salted water according to the instructions on the package.

2 Meanwhile, melt the butter gently in a saucepan, stir in the prosciutto strips and heat through over very gentle heat, being careful not to fry.

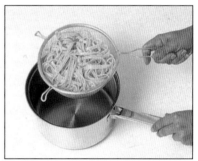

3 Drain the tagliatelle through a colander and pile into a warmed serving dish.

4 Sprinkle on all the Parmesan cheese and pour on the buttery prosciutto. Season well with black pepper and garnish the tagliatelle with the sage leaves.

Spaghetti with Meatballs

No Italian menu would be complete without meatballs. Serve these with a light green salad, if you like.

Serves 4

For the meatballs

1 onion, chopped

1 garlic clove, chopped

3 cups ground lamb

1 egg yolk

1 tablespoon dried mixed herbs

1 tablespoon olive oil

salt and ground black pepper

1¼ cups strained tomatoes

2 tablespoons chopped fresh basil

1 garlic clove, chopped

salt and ground black pepper

12 ounces spaghetti

fresh rosemary sprigs, to garnish

freshly grated Parmesan cheese, to serve

1 To make the meatballs, mix together the onion, garlic, lamb, egg yolk, herbs and seasoning until well blended.

2 Divide the mixture into about 20 pieces and shape into balls. Place on a baking sheet, cover with plastic wrap and chill for at least 30 minutes.

3 Heat the oil in a large frying pan and add the meatballs. Fry for about 10 minutes, turning occasionally, until browned.

4 Add the tomatoes, basil, garlic and seasoning to the pan and bring to a boil. Cover and simmer for 20 minutes, or until the meatballs are tender.

5 Meanwhile, cook the pasta in plenty of boiling salted water according to the instructions on the package. Drain thoroughly and divide among four serving plates. Spoon the meatballs and some of the sauce on top. Garnish each portion with a fresh rosemary sprig and serve immediately with plenty of freshly grated Parmesan cheese passed around separately.

Greek Pasta Bake

*Another excellent main meal (called
pastitsio in Greece), this recipe is
both economical and filling.*

INGREDIENTS

Serves 4

1 tablespoon oil

4 cups ground lamb

1 onion, chopped

2 garlic cloves, crushed

2 tablespoons tomato paste

2 tablespoons all-purpose flour

1¼ cups lamb stock

2 large tomatoes

1 cup pasta shapes

1-pound tub strained yogurt

2 eggs

salt and ground black pepper

1 Preheat the oven to 375°F. Heat
the oil in a large pan and fry
the lamb for 5 minutes. Add the
onion and garlic and continue to
fry for 5 minutes.

2 Stir the tomato paste and flour
into the pan. Cook for
1 minute more.

3 Stir in the stock, and season to
taste. Bring to a boil and cook
for 20 minutes.

4 Slice the tomatoes, place the
meat in a casserole and
arrange the tomatoes on top.

5 Cook the pasta shapes in
boiling salted water for about
8–10 minutes or until *al dente*.
Drain thoroughly.

6 Mix together the pasta, yogurt
and eggs. Spoon on top of the
tomatoes and then cook in the
preheated oven for 1 hour. Serve
with a crisp salad, if liked.

Bolognese Meat Sauce

This great meat sauce is a specialty of Bologna. It is delicious with tagliatelle or short pastas such as penne or conchiglie as well as spaghetti, and is indispensable in baked lasagne. It keeps well in the fridge for several days and can also be frozen for up to three months.

INGREDIENTS

Serves 6

2 tablespoons butter

4 tablespoons olive oil

1 onion, finely chopped

2 tablespoons finely chopped pancetta or unsmoked bacon

1 carrot, finely sliced

1 celery stalk, finely sliced

1 garlic clove, finely chopped

3 cups lean ground beef

⅔ cup red wine

½ cup milk

14-ounce can plum tomatoes, chopped, with their juice

1 bay leaf

¼ teaspoon fresh thyme leaves

salt and ground black pepper

cooked pasta, to serve

1 Heat the butter and oil in a heavy-bottomed saucepan. Add the onion, and cook over medium heat for 3–4 minutes. Add the pancetta or bacon, and cook until the onion is translucent. Stir in the carrot, celery and garlic. Cook for 3–4 minutes more.

2 Add the beef, and crumble it into the vegetables with a fork. Stir until the meat loses its red color. Season to taste.

3 Pour in the wine, increase the heat slightly, and cook until the liquid evaporates, 3–4 minutes. Add the milk and cook until it has evaporated.

4 Stir in the tomatoes with their juice, and the herbs. Bring the sauce to a boil. Reduce the heat to low and simmer, uncovered, for 1½–2 hours, stirring occasionally. Correct the seasoning before serving on a bed of pasta.

Baked Lasagne with Meat Sauce

This lasagne, made from egg pasta with homemade meat and béchamel sauces, is exquisite.

INGREDIENTS

Serves 8–10

2 quantities Bolognese Meat Sauce
egg pasta sheets made with 3 eggs or
   14 ounces dried lasagne
1 cup grated Parmesan cheese
3 tablespoons butter

For the béchamel sauce
3 cups milk
1 bay leaf
3 mace blades
½ cup butter
¾ cup all-purpose flour
salt and ground black pepper

1 Prepare the meat sauce and set aside. Butter a large, shallow casserole, preferably either rectangular or square.

COOK'S TIP
~

If you are using dried or bought pasta, follow step 4, but boil the lasagne in two batches, and stop the cooking about 4 minutes before the recommended cooking time on the package has elapsed. Rinse in cold water and lay the pasta out the same way as for the egg pasta.

---

2 Make the béchamel sauce by gently heating the milk with the bay leaf and mace in a small saucepan. Melt the butter in a medium heavy-bottomed pan. Add the flour, and mix well with a wire whisk. Cook for 2–3 minutes. Strain the hot milk into the flour and butter, and mix smoothly with the whisk. Bring the sauce to a boil, stirring constantly, and cook for 4–5 minutes more. Season with salt and pepper and set aside.

3 Make the pasta. Do not let it dry out before cutting it into rectangles measuring about 4½ inches wide and the same length as the casserole (this will make it easier to assemble the lasagne later). Preheat the oven to 400°F.

4 Bring a very large pan of water to a boil. Place a large bowl of cold water near the stove. Cover a work surface with a tablecloth. Add salt to the rapidly boiling water. Drop in 3 or 4 of the egg

pasta rectangles. Cook very briefly, about 30 seconds. Remove from the pan, using a slotted spoon, and drop into the cold water for about 30 seconds. Pull them out of the water, shaking off the excess water. Lay them out flat without overlapping on the tablecloth. Continue with all the remaining pasta and trimmings.

5 To assemble the lasagne, spread one large spoonful of the meat sauce over the bottom of the dish. Arrange a layer of pasta in the dish, cutting it with a sharp knife so that it fits well.

6 Cover with a thin layer of meat sauce, then one of béchamel. Sprinkle with a little cheese. Repeat the layers in the same order, ending with a layer of pasta coated with béchamel. Do not make more than about six layers of pasta. Use the pasta trimmings to patch any gaps in the pasta. Sprinkle the top with grated Parmesan cheese, and dot with butter.

7 Bake in the preheated oven for 20 minutes, or until brown on top. Remove from the oven and let stand for about 5 minutes before serving. Serve directly from the dish, cutting out rectangular or square sections for each helping.

Twin Cities Meatballs

Serve these meatballs without gravy as drinks party nibbles.

INGREDIENTS

Serves 6

2 tablespoons butter or margarine

½ small onion, ground

2¼ cups ground beef

1 cup ground veal

2 cups ground pork

1 egg

½ cup mashed potato

2 tablespoons finely chopped fresh dill
    or parsley

1 garlic clove, crushed

1 teaspoon salt

½ teaspoon black pepper

½ teaspoon ground allspice

¼ teaspoon grated nutmeg

¾ cup fresh bread crumbs

¾ cup milk

¼ cup all-purpose flour, plus
    1 tablespoon extra

2 tablespoons olive oil

¾ cup evaporated milk

buttered noodles, to serve

1 Melt the butter or margarine in a large frying pan. Add the onion and cook over low heat until softened, about 8–10 minutes. Remove from the heat. Using a slotted spoon, transfer the onion to a large mixing bowl.

2 Add the beef, veal and pork, the egg, mashed potato, dill or parsley, garlic, salt, pepper, allspice and nutmeg to the bowl.

3 Put the bread crumbs in a small bowl and add the milk. Stir until well moistened, then add to the other ingredients. Mix well.

4 Shape the mixture into balls about 1 inch in diameter. Roll them in ¼ cup of the flour to coat all over.

5 Add the olive oil to the frying pan and heat over medium heat. Add the meatballs and brown on all sides for 8–10 minutes. Shake the pan occasionally to roll the balls so they color evenly. With a slotted spoon, remove the meatballs to a serving dish. Cover with foil and keep warm.

6 Stir the extra 1 tablespoon of flour into the fat in the frying pan. Add the evaporated milk and mix in with a small whisk. Simmer for 3–4 minutes. Check the seasoning, and adjust if necessary.

7 Pour the gravy over the meatballs. Serve hot with buttered noodles.

Pasta Timbales

An alternative way to serve pasta for a special occasion. Mixed with ground beef and tomato and baked in a lettuce package, it makes an impressive dish for a dinner party.

Serves 4

8 Romaine lettuce leaves

For the filling

1 tablespoon oil

1½ cups ground beef

1 tablespoon tomato paste

1 garlic clove, crushed

4 ounces macaroni

salt and ground black pepper

For the sauce

2 tablespoons butter

2 tablespoons all-purpose flour

1 cup heavy cream

2 tablespoons chopped fresh basil

1 Preheat the oven to 350°F. For the filling, heat the oil in a large pan and fry the ground beef for 7 minutes. Add the tomato paste and garlic and cook for 5 minutes.

2 Cook the macaroni in boiling salted water for 8–10 minutes or until *al dente*. Drain.

3 Mix together the pasta and ground beef mixture.

4 Line four ⅔-cup ramekin dishes with the lettuce leaves. Season the mince and spoon into the lettuce-lined ramekins.

5 Fold the lettuce leaves over the filling and place in a roasting pan half-filled with boiling water. Cover and cook in the oven for 20 minutes.

6 For the sauce, melt the butter in a pan. Add the flour and cook for 1 minute. Stir in the cream and fresh basil. Season and bring to a boil, stirring all the time. Turn out the timbales and serve with the creamy basil sauce, and a crisp, green salad, if liked.

Cannelloni Stuffed with Meat

Cannelloni are rectangles of egg pasta which are spread with a filling, rolled up and baked in a sauce. In this recipe, they are baked in a béchamel sauce.

INGREDIENTS

Serves 6–8

2 tablespoons olive oil

1 onion, very finely chopped

1½ cups very lean ground beef

½ cup finely chopped cooked ham

1 tablespoon chopped fresh parsley

2 tablespoons tomato paste, softened in
   1 tablespoon warm water

1 egg

egg pasta sheets made with 2 eggs

3 cups béchamel sauce

½ cup freshly grated Parmesan cheese

3 tablespoons butter

salt and ground black pepper

1 Prepare the meat filling by heating the oil in a medium saucepan. Add the onion and sauté gently until translucent. Stir in the beef, crumbling it with a fork, and stirring constantly until it has lost its raw, red color. Cook for about 3–4 minutes.

2 Remove from the heat and turn the beef mixture into a bowl with the ham and parsley. Add the tomato paste mixture and the egg, and mix well. Season with salt and pepper. Set aside.

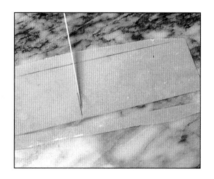

3 Make the egg pasta sheets. Do not let the pasta dry before cutting it into rectangles, about 5–6 inches long and as wide as they come from the machine (3 inches if you are not using a pasta machine).

4 Bring a very large pan of water to a boil. Place a large bowl of cold water near the stove. Cover a work surface with a tablecloth. Add salt to the rapidly boiling water. Drop in three or four of the egg pasta rectangles. Cook very briefly, for about 30 seconds. Plunge them into the cold water, shake off the excess and lay them out flat on the tablecloth. Continue until all the pasta has been cooked in this way.

5 Preheat the oven to 425°F. Select a shallow casserole large enough to take all the cannelloni in one layer. Butter the casserole and smear about 2–3 tablespoons of béchamel sauce over the bottom.

6 Stir about a third of the sauce into the meat filling. Spread a thin layer of filling on each pasta rectangle. Roll the rectangles up loosely starting from a long side, jelly roll style. Place the cannelloni in the casserole with their open edges underneath.

7 Spoon the rest of the sauce over the cannelloni, pushing a little down between each pasta roll. Sprinkle the top with the grated Parmesan and dot with butter. Bake for about 20 minutes. Let rest for 5–8 minutes before serving on warmed plates.

Beef Strips with Orange and Ginger

Stir-frying is one of the quickest ways to cook, but you do need to choose tender meat.

INGREDIENTS

Serves 4

1 pound lean beef round steak, fillet or
   sirloin, cut into thin strips
finely grated rind and juice of 1 orange
1 tablespoon light soy sauce
1 teaspoon cornstarch
1-inch piece fresh ginger, finely chopped
2 teaspoons sesame oil
1 large carrot, cut into thin strips
2 scallions, thinly sliced
rice noodles, to serve

1 Place the beef strips in a bowl and sprinkle on the orange rind and juice. Let marinate for at least 30 minutes.

2 Drain the liquid from the meat and reserve, then mix the meat with the soy sauce, cornstarch and fresh ginger.

3 Heat the oil in a wok or large frying pan and add the beef. Stir-fry for 1 minute until lightly colored, then add the carrot and stir-fry for 2–3 minutes more.

4 Stir in the scallions and reserved liquid, then cook, stirring, until boiling and thickened. Serve the beef hot with rice noodles.

Piquant Chicken with Spaghetti

The addition of cucumber and tomatoes adds a deliciously fresh flavor to this unusual dish.

INGREDIENTS

Serves 4

1 onion, finely chopped

1 carrot, diced

1 garlic clove, crushed

1¼ cups vegetable stock

4 chicken breasts, boned and skinned

1 bouquet garni

4 ounces button mushrooms, thinly sliced

1 teaspoon wine vinegar or lemon juice

12 ounces spaghetti

½ cucumber, peeled and cut into fingers

2 tomatoes, skinned, seeded and chopped

2 tablespoons crème fraîche

1 tablespoon chopped fresh parsley

1 tablespoon chopped chives

salt and ground black pepper

1 Put the onion, carrot, garlic, stock, chicken and bouquet garni into a saucepan.

2 Bring to a boil, cover and simmer for 15–20 minutes or until the chicken is tender. Transfer the chicken to a plate and cover with foil.

3 Remove the chicken and strain the liquid. Discard the vegetables and return the liquid to the pan. Add the sliced mushrooms, wine vinegar or lemon juice and simmer for 2–3 minutes.

4 Cook the spaghetti in plenty of boiling salted water according to the instructions on the package. Drain well.

5 Blanch the cucumber in boiling water for 10 seconds. Drain and rinse under cold water.

6 Cut the chicken breasts into bite-size pieces. Boil the stock to reduce by half, then add the chicken, tomatoes, crème fraîche, cucumber and herbs. Season with salt and pepper to taste.

7 Transfer the spaghetti to a warmed serving dish and spoon on the piquant chicken. Serve immediately.

Chicken Cannelloni al Forno

A lighter alternative to the usual beef-filled, béchamel-coated version. Fill with ricotta cheese, onion and mushroom for a vegetarian version.

INGREDIENTS

Serves 4–6

1 pound skinless, boneless chicken breast, cooked

3 cups baby mushrooms

2 garlic cloves, crushed

2 tablespoons chopped fresh parsley

1 tablespoons chopped fresh tarragon

1 egg, beaten

freshly squeezed lemon juice

12-18 cannelloni tubes

14oz jar tomato pasta sauce

½ cup freshly grated Parmesan cheese

salt and ground black pepper

fresh parsley sprig, to garnish

1 Preheat the oven to 400°F. Place the chicken in a blender or food processor and process until finely ground. Transfer to a bowl.

2 Place the mushrooms, garlic, parsley and tarragon in the blender or food processor and process until finely ground.

3 Beat the mushroom mixture into the chicken with the egg, salt and ground black pepper, and lemon juice to taste.

4 If necessary, cook the cannelloni in plenty of salted boiling water according to the instructions on the package. Drain well and pat dry on a clean dish towel.

5 Place the filling in a pastry bag fitted with a large, plain tip. Use to fill each tube of cannelloni.

6 Lay the filled cannelloni tightly together in a single layer in a buttered shallow casserole. Spoon the tomato sauce over them and sprinkle with Parmesan cheese. Bake in the oven for 30 minutes, or until brown and bubbling. Serve the cannelloni garnished with a sprig of parsley.

Chicken Lasagne

Based on the Italian beef lasagne, this is an excellent dish for entertaining guests of all ages. Serve simply with a green salad.

Serves 8

2 tablespoons olive oil

8 cups ground raw chicken

8 ounces rindless lean bacon strips, chopped

2 garlic cloves, crushed

4 cups sliced leeks

1¼ cups diced carrots

2 tablespoons tomato paste

1¾ cups chicken stock

12 sheets (no-precook) green lasagne

For the cheese sauce

4 tablespoons butter

4 tablespoons all-purpose flour

2½ cups milk

1 cup grated aged Cheddar cheese

¼ teaspoon English mustard powder

salt and ground black pepper

1 Heat the oil in a large flame-proof casserole and brown the ground chicken and bacon briskly, separating the pieces with a wooden spoon. Add the crushed garlic cloves, sliced leeks and diced carrots and cook for about 5 minutes until softened. Add the tomato paste, stock and seasoning. Bring to a boil, cover and simmer for 30 minutes.

2 For the sauce, melt the butter in a saucepan, add the flour and gradually blend in the milk, stirring until smooth. Bring to a boil, stirring all the time until thickened, and simmer for several minutes. Add half the grated Cheddar cheese and the mustard. Season to taste.

3 Preheat the oven to 375°F. Layer the chicken mixture, lasagne and half the cheese sauce in a 12-cup casserole, starting and finishing with the chicken mixture.

4 Pour on the remaining cheese sauce, sprinkle on the remaining cheese and bake in the preheated oven for 1 hour, or until lightly browned.

Noodles with Chicken, Shrimp and Ham

Unlike most other kinds of noodle, egg noodles can be cooked up to 24 hours in advance and kept in a bowl of cold water in the refrigerator until required.

INGREDIENTS

Serves 4–6

10 ounces dried egg noodles

1 tablespoon vegetable oil

1 medium onion, chopped

1 clove garlic, crushed

1-inch piece fresh ginger
    root, chopped

2 ounces canned water chestnuts,
    drained, rinsed and sliced

1 tablespoon light soy sauce

2 tablespoons fish sauce or strong
    chicken stock

6 ounces cooked boneless chicken
    breast, thinly sliced

5 ounces cooked ham, thickly sliced
    and cut into short fingers

8 ounces cooked shrimp, peeled

6 ounces bean sprouts

7 ounce can baby corn cobs,
    drained

2 limes, cut into wedges, and 1 small
    bunch cilantro, shredded,
    to garnish

1 Cook the noodles according to the packet instructions. Drain well and set aside.

2 Heat the oil in a preheated wok or heavy-based skillet. Add the onion, garlic and ginger and stir-fry for 3 minutes, until the onion is soft but not colored. Add the chestnuts, soy sauce, fish sauce or chicken stock, chicken breast, ham and shrimp.

3 Add the drained egg noodles, bean sprouts and baby corn cobs and stir-fry for about 6–8 minutes, until thoroughly heated through. Transfer to a warm serving dish, garnish with the lime wedges and shredded cilantro, and serve immediately.

Stir-fried Sweet and Sour Chicken

There are few cookery concepts that are better suited to today's busy lifestyle than the all-in-one stir-fry. This one has a wonderful southeast Asian influence.

INGREDIENTS

Serves 4

10 ounces Chinese egg noodles

2 tablespoons vegetable oil

3 scallions, chopped

1 garlic clove, crushed

1-inch piece fresh ginger, peeled and grated

1 teaspoon hot paprika

1 teaspoon ground coriander

3 boneless chicken breasts, sliced

1 cup sugar snap peas, ends removed

4 ounces baby corn, halved

1 cup fresh bean sprouts

1 tablespoon cornstarch

3 tablespoons soy sauce

3 tablespoons lemon juice

1 tablespoon sugar

3 tablespoons chopped fresh cilantro or scallion tops, to garnish

1 Bring a large saucepan of salted water to a boil. Add the noodles and cook according to the instructions on the package. Drain, cover and keep warm.

2 Heat the oil in a wok. Add the scallions and cook over gentle heat. Mix in the next five ingredients, then stir-fry for about 3–4 minutes. Add the next three ingredients and steam briefly. Add the noodles.

3 Combine the cornstarch, soy sauce, lemon juice and sugar in a small bowl. Add to the wok and simmer briefly to thicken. Serve garnished with chopped cilantro or scallion tops.

VEGETARIAN
DISHES

Pasta with Caponata

*The Sicilians have an excellent
sweet-and-sour vegetable dish,
called* caponata, *which goes
wonderfully well with pasta.*

INGREDIENTS

Serves 4

1 eggplant, cut into sticks

2 zucchini, cut into sticks

8 baby onions, peeled, or 1 large
    onion, sliced

2 garlic cloves, crushed

1 large red bell pepper, sliced

4 tablespoons olive oil, preferably
    extra virgin

1¾ cups tomato juice

⅔ cup water

2 tablespoons balsamic vinegar

juice of 1 lemon

1 tablespoon sugar

2 tablespoons sliced black olives

2 tablespoons capers

14 ounces tagliatelle or other
    ribbon pasta

salt and ground black pepper

1 Lightly salt the eggplant and
zucchini and let them drain in
a colander for 30 minutes. Rinse
and pat dry with paper towels.

2 In a large saucepan, lightly fry
the onions, garlic and bell
pepper in the oil for 5 minutes,
then stir in the eggplant and
zucchini and fry for 5 minutes.

3 Stir in the tomato juice and
water. Stir well, bring the
mixture to a boil, then add all the
rest of the ingredients except the
pasta. Season to taste and simmer
for 10 minutes.

4 Meanwhile, cook the pasta
according to the instructions
on the package, then drain. Serve
the *caponata* with the pasta.

Eggplant Lasagne

*This delicious lasagne is also
suitable for home freezing.*

Serves 4

3 eggplant, sliced

5 tablespoons olive oil

2 large onions, finely chopped

2 × 14-ounce cans chopped tomatoes

1 teaspoon dried mixed herbs

2–3 garlic cloves, crushed

6 sheets no-precook lasagne

salt and ground black pepper

For the cheese sauce

2 tablespoons butter

2 tablespoons all-purpose flour

1¼ cups milk

½ teaspoon English mustard

8 tablespoons grated aged Cheddar

1 tablespoon grated Parmesan cheese

1 Layer the sliced eggplant in a
colander, sprinkling lightly
with salt between each layer. Let
stand for 1 hour, then rinse and
pat dry with paper towels.

2 Heat 4 tablespoons of the oil in
a large pan, fry the eggplant
and drain on paper towels. Add the
remaining oil to the pan, cook the
onions for 5 minutes, then stir in
the tomatoes, herbs, garlic and
seasoning. Bring to a boil and
simmer, covered, for 30 minutes.

3 Melt the butter in a pan, stir in
the flour and cook gently for
1 minute, stirring. Gradually stir in
the milk. Bring to a boil, stirring,
and cook for 2 minutes. Remove
from the heat and stir in the
mustard, cheeses and seasoning.

4 Preheat the oven to 400°F.
Arrange half the eggplant in
the bottom of a casserole and
spoon on half the tomato sauce.
Arrange three sheets of lasagne on
top. Repeat.

5 Spoon on the cheese sauce,
cover and bake for 30 minutes,
until lightly browned.

Spaghetti with Mixed Mushrooms

This combination of mixed mushrooms and freshly chopped sweet basil tossed with spaghetti would be well complemented by a simple tomato salad.

INGREDIENTS

Serves 4

¼ cup butter

1 onion, chopped

12 ounces spaghetti

12 ounces mixed mushrooms, such as
    brown, flat and button, sliced

1 garlic clove, chopped

1¼ cups sour cream

2 tablespoons chopped fresh basil

½ cup freshly grated Parmesan cheese

salt and ground black pepper

torn Italian parsley, to garnish

freshly grated Parmesan cheese, to serve

1 Melt the butter in a large frying pan and fry the chopped onion for 10 minutes until softened.

2 Cook the pasta in plenty of boiling salted water according to the instructions on the package.

5 Drain the pasta thoroughly and toss with the sauce. Serve immediately, garnished with torn Italian parsley, with plenty of grated Parmesan cheese.

3 Stir the mushrooms and garlic into the onion mixture and fry for 10 minutes until softened.

4 Add the sour cream, basil, grated Parmesan cheese and salt and pepper to taste. Cover and heat through.

Tortelli with Pumpkin Stuffing

During fall and winter, the northern Italian markets are full of bright orange pumpkins that are used to make soups and pasta dishes. This flavorsome dish is a specialty of Mantua.

INGREDIENTS

Serves 6-8

2¼ pounds pumpkin (weight with shell)

1½ cups amaretti cookies, crushed

2 eggs

¾ cup freshly grated Parmesan cheese

pinch of grated nutmeg

plain bread crumbs, as required

egg pasta sheets made with 3 eggs

salt and ground black pepper

To serve

½ cup butter

¾ cup freshly grated Parmesan cheese

1 Preheat the oven to 375°F. Cut the pumpkin into 4-inch pieces, leaving the skin on. Place the pumpkin pieces in a covered casserole and bake for about 45–50 minutes. When cool, cut off the skins. Process the flesh in a food mill, blender or food processor or press through a strainer with a wooden spoon.

2 Combine the pumpkin paste with the cookie crumbs, eggs, Parmesan and nutmeg. Season with salt and pepper. If the mixture is too wet, add 1–2 table-spoons bread crumbs. Set aside until required.

3 Prepare the sheets of egg pasta. Roll out very thinly by hand or machine. Do not let the pasta dry out before filling.

4 Place tablespoonfuls of filling every 2½ inches along the pasta in rows 2 inches apart. Cover with another sheet of pasta, and press down gently. Use a fluted pastry or pasta wheel to cut between the rows to form rectangles with filling in the center of each. Place the tortelli on a lightly floured surface, and let dry for at least 30 minutes, turning occasionally to dry both sides.

5 Bring a large pan of salted water to a boil. Gently heat the butter over very low heat, taking care that it does not darken.

6 Drop the tortelli into the boiling water. Stir to prevent them from sticking. They will be cooked in 4–5 minutes. Drain and arrange in individual dishes. Spoon the melted butter on top, sprinkle with grated Parmesan cheese and serve immediately.

Magnificent Large Zucchini

At fall time, large zucchini or squashes – with their wonderful colors – look so attractive and tempting. They make delicious, inexpensive main courses, perfect for a satisfying family meal.

INGREDIENTS

Serves 4–6

9 ounces pasta shells

3–4½ pounds large zucchini

1 onion, chopped

1 bell pepper, seeded and chopped

1 tablespoon grated fresh ginger root

2 garlic cloves, crushed

3 tablespoons sunflower oil

4 large tomatoes, skinned and chopped

½ cup pine nuts

1 tablespoon chopped fresh basil

salt and ground black pepper

grated cheese, to serve (optional)

1 Preheat the oven to 375°F. Cook the pasta in plenty of boiling salted water according to the instructions on the package, slightly overcooking it so it is just a little soft. Drain well and reserve.

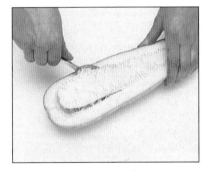

2 Cut the zucchini in half lengthwise and scoop out and discard the seeds. Use a small, sharp knife and tablespoon to scoop out the flesh. Chop it coarsely.

3 Gently fry the onion, bell pepper, ginger and garlic in the oil for 5 minutes, then add the zucchini flesh, tomatoes and seasoning. Cover and cook for 10–12 minutes, or until the vegetables are soft.

4 Add the pasta, pine nuts and basil to the pan, stir well and set aside until required.

5 Meanwhile, place the zucchini halves in a roasting pan, season lightly and pour a little water around, taking care it does not spill inside the zucchini. Cover with foil and bake for 15 minutes.

6 Remove the foil, discard the water and fill the shells with the vegetable mixture. Cover with foil and return to the oven for 20–25 minutes more.

7 Top with cheese, if using. To serve, scoop out of the "shell" or cut into sections.

Cilantro Ravioli with Pumpkin Filling

This stunning herb pasta is served with a superb, creamy pumpkin and roast garlic filling.

INGREDIENTS

Serves 4–6

scant 1 cup white bread flour

2 eggs

pinch of salt

3 tablespoons chopped fresh cilantro

cilantro sprigs, to garnish

For the filling

4 garlic cloves, unpeeled

1 pound pumpkin, peeled and seeded

½ cup ricotta cheese

4 sun-dried tomatoes in olive oil, drained
    and finely chopped, and
    2 tablespoons of the oil

ground black pepper

1 Place the flour, eggs, salt and chopped fresh cilantro into a blender or food processor and process until combined.

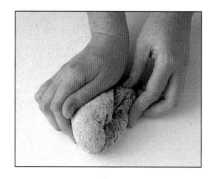

2 Place the dough on a lightly floured board and knead well for 5 minutes, until smooth. Wrap in plastic wrap and let rest in the fridge for 20 minutes.

3 Preheat the oven to 400°F. Place the garlic cloves on a baking sheet and bake for about 10 minutes until soft. Steam the pumpkin for 5–8 minutes until tender and drain well. Peel the garlic cloves and mash into the pumpkin together with the ricotta cheese and drained sun-dried tomatoes. Season with lots of ground black pepper.

4 Divide the pasta into four pieces and flatten slightly. Using a pasta machine on its thinnest setting, roll out each piece. Let the sheets of pasta rest on a clean dish towel until they are slightly dried.

5 Using a 3-inch crinkle-edged round cutter, stamp out 36 rounds of pasta.

6 Top 18 of the rounds with a teaspoonful of filling, brush the edges with water and place another round of pasta on top. Press firmly around the edges to seal. Bring a large pan of water to a boil, add the ravioli and cook for 3–4 minutes. Drain well and toss into the reserved tomato oil. Serve immediately garnished with fresh cilantro sprigs.

Fall Glory

Glorious pumpkin shells summon up the delights of fall and seem too good simply to throw away. Use one instead as a serving dish. Pumpkin and pasta make marvelous partners, particularly as a main course served from the baked shell.

INGREDIENTS

Serves 4

4–4½ pounds pumpkin

1 onion, sliced

1-inch piece fresh ginger

3 tablespoons extra virgin olive oil

1 zucchini, sliced

4 ounces sliced mushrooms

14-ounce can chopped tomatoes

3 ounces pasta shells

1¾ cups stock

4 tablespoons ricotta cheese

2 tablespoons chopped fresh basil

salt and ground black pepper

1 Preheat the oven to 350°F. Cut the top off the pumpkin with a large, sharp knife and scoop out and discard the pumpkin seeds.

2 Using a small, sharp knife and a sturdy tablespoon, cut and scrape out as much flesh from the pumpkin shell as possible, then chop the flesh into coarse chunks.

3 Bake the pumpkin shell with its lid on for 45 minutes–1 hour until the inside begins to soften.

4 Meanwhile, make the filling. Gently fry the onion, ginger and pumpkin flesh in the olive oil for about 10 minutes, stirring the mixture occasionally.

5 Add the sliced zucchini and mushrooms and cook for 3 minutes more, then stir in the tomatoes, pasta shells and stock. Season well, bring to a boil, then cover the pan and simmer gently for about 10 minutes.

6 Stir the ricotta cheese and basil into the pasta and spoon the mixture into the pumpkin. It may not be possible to fit all the filling into the pumpkin shell, so serve the rest separately, if necessary.

Stuffed Pasta Half-moons

These stuffed egg pasta half-moons are filled with a delicate mixture of cheeses. They make an elegant first course as well as a good supper.

INGREDIENTS

Serves 6–8

1¼ cups fresh ricotta or curd cheese

1¼ cups chopped mozzarella cheese

1 cup freshly grated Parmesan cheese

2 eggs

3 tablespoons finely chopped fresh basil

salt and ground black pepper

egg pasta sheets made with 3 eggs

For the sauce

1 pound fresh tomatoes

2 tablespoons olive oil

1 small onion, very finely chopped

6 tablespoons cream

1 Press the ricotta or curd cheese through a strainer. Chop the mozzarella into very small cubes. Combine all three cheeses in a bowl. Beat in the eggs and basil, season and set aside.

2 Drop the tomatoes into a small pan of boiling water for 1 minute and then into cold water. Remove, and peel using a small, sharp knife to pull off the skins. Chop the tomatoes finely. Heat the oil in a medium saucepan. Add the onion and cook over medium heat until soft and translucent. Add the tomatoes and cook until soft, about 15 minutes. Season with salt and pepper. (The sauce may be pressed through a strainer to make it smooth.) Set aside.

3 Prepare the sheets of egg pasta. Roll out very thinly by hand or machine. Do not let the pasta dry out before filling.

4 Using a glass or pastry cutter, cut out rounds 4 inches in diameter. Spoon one large tablespoon of the cheese filling onto one half of each pasta round and fold over.

5 Press the edges closed with a fork. Re-roll any trimmings and use to make more rounds. Let the half-moons dry for at least 10–15 minutes. Turn them over so they dry evenly.

6 Bring a large pan of salted water to a boil. Meanwhile, place the tomato sauce in a small saucepan and heat gently. Stir in the cream. Do not allow to boil.

7 Gently drop the stuffed pasta in the boiling water, and stir carefully to prevent them from sticking. Cook for 5–7 minutes. Scoop them out of the water, drain carefully, and arrange in individual dishes. Spoon on some sauce to serve.

Baked Vegetable Lasagne

Following the principles of the classic meat sauce lasagne, other combinations of ingredients can be used most effectively. This vegetarian lasagne uses tomatoes and wild and cultivated mushrooms.

INGREDIENTS

Serves 8

egg pasta sheets made with 3 eggs

2 tablespoons olive oil

1 onion, very finely chopped

1¼ pounds tomatoes, fresh or
    canned, chopped

1½ pounds cultivated or wild
    mushrooms, or a mixture

⅓ cup butter

2 garlic cloves, finely chopped

juice of ½ lemon

4 cups béchamel sauce

salt and ground black pepper

1½ cups freshly grated Parmesan or
    Cheddar cheese, or a mixture

1 Butter a large, shallow casserole, preferably rectangular or square in shape.

2 Make the egg pasta. Do not let it dry out before cutting it into rectangles about 4½ inches wide and the same length as the casserole (this makes the lasagne easier to assemble).

3 In a small frying pan, heat the oil and sauté the onion until translucent. Add the chopped tomatoes and cook for about 6–8 minutes, stirring often. Season with salt and pepper and set aside until required.

4 Wipe the mushrooms carefully with a damp cloth and slice finely. Heat 3 tablespoons of the butter in a frying pan and, when it is bubbling, add the mushrooms. Cook until the mushrooms start to exude their juices. Add the garlic and lemon juice, and season with salt and pepper. Cook until the liquids have almost all evaporated and the mushrooms are starting to brown. Set aside.

5 Preheat the oven to 400°F. Bring a very large pan of water to a boil. Place a large bowl of cold water near the stove. Cover a work surface with a tablecloth. Add salt to the rapidly boiling water. Drop in three or four of the egg pasta rectangles. Cook very briefly, about 30 seconds. Remove from the pan with a slotted spoon and drop into the cold water for 30 seconds. Remove and lay out to dry. Continue with the remaining pasta rectangles.

6 To assemble the lasagne, spread one large spoonful of the béchamel sauce over the bottom of the casserole. Arrange a layer of pasta in the dish, cutting it with a sharp knife to fit. Cover with a thin layer of mushrooms, then one of béchamel sauce. Sprinkle with a little cheese.

7 Make another layer of pasta, spread with a thin layer of tomatoes, and then one of béchamel. Sprinkle with cheese. Repeat the layers in the same order, ending with a layer of pasta coated with béchamel. Do not make more than about six layers of pasta. Use the pasta trimmings to patch any gaps in the pasta. Sprinkle with more cheese and dot with butter.

8 Bake for 20 minutes. Remove from the oven and let stand for 5 minutes before serving.

Leek and Chèvre Lasagne

An unusual and lighter than average lasagne using a soft French goat cheese. The pasta sheets are not so chewy if boiled briefly first, or you could use no-precook lasagne instead, if you prefer.

INGREDIENTS

Serves 6

6–8 lasagne sheets

1 large eggplant, sliced

3 leeks, thinly sliced

2 tablespoons olive oil

2 red bell peppers, roasted

7 ounces goat cheese, broken into pieces

½ cup freshly grated pecorino or
    Parmesan cheese

For the sauce

9 tablespoons all-purpose flour

5 tablespoons butter

3¾ cups milk

½ teaspoon ground bay leaves

freshly grated nutmeg

salt and ground black pepper

1 Blanch the pasta sheets in plenty of boiling water for just 2 minutes. Drain and place on a clean dish towel.

2 Lightly salt the eggplant slices and place in a colander to drain for 30 minutes, then rinse and pat dry with paper towels.

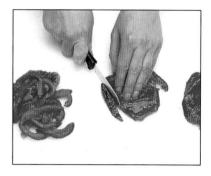

3 Preheat the oven to 375°F. Lightly fry the leeks in the oil for 5 minutes, until softened. Peel the roasted bell peppers and cut them into strips.

4 To make the sauce, put the flour, butter and milk into a saucepan and bring to a boil, stirring constantly until thickened. Add the ground bay leaves, nutmeg and seasoning. Simmer the sauce for 2 minutes.

5 In a greased, shallow casserole, layer the leeks, lasagne sheets, eggplant, goat cheese and pecorino or Parmesan. Trickle the sauce over the layers, making sure that plenty goes in between.

6 Finish with a layer of sauce and grated cheese. Bake in the oven for 30 minutes, or until bubbling and browned on top. Serve immediately.

Pasta with Roasted Vegetables

Sweet, roasted vegetables form the basis of a rich sauce.

Serves 4

1 large onion

1 eggplant

2 zucchini

2 red or yellow bell peppers, seeded

1 pound tomatoes, preferably plum

2-3 garlic cloves, coarsely chopped

4 tablespoons olive oil

1¼ cups smooth tomato sauce

2 ounces black olives, pitted and halved

12 ounces-1 pound dried pasta shapes,
   such as rigatoni or penne

salt and ground black pepper

½ ounce fresh basil, shredded, to garnish

freshly grated Parmesan or pecorino
   cheese, to serve

1 Preheat the oven to 475°F. Cut the onion, eggplant, zucchini, bell peppers and tomatoes into 1–1½ inch chunks. Scoop out and discard the tomato seeds.

2 Spread out the vegetables in a large roasting pan. Sprinkle the garlic and oil over the vegetables and stir and turn to mix evenly. Season with salt and pepper.

3 Roast the vegetables for about 30 minutes, or until they are soft and browned (don't worry if the edges are charred black). Stir after 15 minutes.

4 Scrape the vegetable mixture into a saucepan. Add the tomato sauce and olives.

5 Cook the pasta in plenty of boiling salted water, according to the instructions on the package, until *al dente*.

6 Meanwhile, heat the tomato and roasted vegetable sauce. Taste and adjust the seasoning, if necessary.

7 Drain the pasta and return to the pan. Add the tomato and roasted vegetable sauce and stir to mix well. Serve hot, sprinkled with the basil. If you like, serve the dish with freshly grated Parmesan or pecorino cheese passed separately.

Penne with Eggplant and Mint Pesto

This splendid variation on the classic Italian pesto uses fresh mint rather than basil for a deliciously different flavor.

INGREDIENTS

Serves 4

2 large eggplant

1 pound penne

½ cup walnut halves

salt and ground black pepper

For the pesto

1 ounce fresh mint

½ ounce Italian parsley

scant ½ cup walnuts

1½ ounces finely grated Parmesan cheese

2 garlic cloves

6 tablespoons olive oil

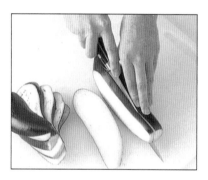

1 Cut the eggplant lengthwise into ½-inch slices.

2 Cut the slices again crosswise to give short strips.

3 Layer the strips in a colander with salt and let stand for about 30 minutes over a plate to catch any juices. Rinse well in cool water and then drain thoroughly.

4 Place all the pesto ingredients, except the oil, in a blender or food processor. Blend until very smooth, then gradually add the oil in a thin stream until the mixture amalgamates. Season to taste.

5 Cook the penne in plenty of boiling salted water according to the instructions on the package, for about 8 minutes or until *al dente*. Add the eggplant and cook for 3 minutes more.

6 Drain the pasta well and mix in the mint pesto and walnut halves. Serve immediately.

Macaroni Soufflé

This is generally a great favorite with children, and is rather like a light and fluffy macaroni cheese. Make sure you serve the soufflé immediately after it is cooked or it will sink dramatically.

INGREDIENTS

Serves 3–4

3 ounces short cut macaroni

melted butter, to coat

3 tablespoons dried bread crumbs

4 tablespoons butter

1 teaspoon ground paprika

⅓ cup all-purpose flour

1¼ cups milk

¾ cup Cheddar or Gruyère cheese, grated

¾ cup Parmesan cheese, grated

3 eggs, separated

salt and ground black pepper

1 Cook the macaroni in plenty of boiling salted water according to the instructions on the package. Drain well and set aside. Preheat the oven to 300°F.

2 Brush a 5-cup soufflé dish with melted butter, then coat evenly with the bread crumbs, shaking out any excess from the pan.

3 Put the butter, paprika, flour and milk into a saucepan and slowly bring to a boil, whisking constantly until the mixture is smooth and thick.

4 Simmer the sauce gently for 1 minute, then remove from the heat and stir in the cheeses until melted. Season well and mix with the cooked macaroni.

5 Beat in the egg yolks. Whisk the egg whites until they form soft peaks and stir a quarter into the sauce mixture to lighten it slightly.

6 Using a large, metal spoon, carefully fold in the rest of the egg whites and transfer to the prepared soufflé dish.

7 Bake in the center of the oven for about 40–45 minutes, until the soufflé is risen and golden brown. The middle should wobble very slightly and the soufflé should be lightly creamy inside.

Ravioli with Cheese and Herbs

Vary the herbs according to what you have to hand.

INGREDIENTS

Serves 4–6

1 cup full-fat cream cheese, softened
1 garlic clove, finely chopped
1 ounce mixed herbs, such as thyme, basil, chives and parsley, finely chopped
1 quantity fresh pasta dough, rolled by machine into 2 x 12-inch strips, or divided into 4 and rolled by hand as thinly as possible
semolina, to coat
½ cup butter
salt and ground black pepper

1 Mix together the cream cheese, garlic and most of the herbs. Season with salt and pepper.

2 Make the ravioli, filling them with the cheese and herb mixture. Toss the ravioli in a little semolina to coat lightly and let rest at room temperature for about 15 minutes.

3 Bring a large pan of salted water to a boil. Drop in the ravioli and cook for 7–9 minutes or until they are just tender to the bite. Drain well.

4 Melt the butter. Toss the ravioli in the melted butter. Sprinkle with the remaining herbs and serve immediately.

VARIATION

For Ravioli with Gorgonzola and Pine Nuts, fill the ravioli with a mixture of ½ cup each full-fat cream cheese and crumbled Gorgonzola cheese; omit the garlic and herbs. Sprinkle the cooked ravioli with ¼ cup toasted pine nuts instead of herbs.

Baked Tortellini with Three Cheeses

Serve this straight out of the oven while the cheese is still runny. If smoked mozzarella cheese is not available, try using a smoked German cheese or even grated smoked Cheddar.

INGREDIENTS

Serves 4–6

1 pound fresh tortellini

2 eggs

1½ cups ricotta or curd cheese

2 tablespoons butter

1 ounce fresh basil leaves

4 ounces smoked mozzarella cheese

4 tablespoons freshly grated
   Parmesan cheese

salt and ground black pepper

1 Preheat the oven to 375°F. Cook the fresh tortellini in plenty of boiling salted water according to the instructions on the package. Drain well.

2 Beat the eggs with the ricotta or curd cheese and season well with salt and pepper. Use the butter to grease a casserole. Spoon in half the tortellini, pour on half the cheese mixture and cover with half the basil leaves.

3 Cover with the mozzarella and remaining basil. Top with the rest of the tortellini and spread over the remaining ricotta or curd cheese mixture.

4 Sprinkle evenly with the Parmesan cheese. Bake in the oven for 35–45 minutes, or until golden brown and bubbling.

SALADS

Pasta Salad with Olives

This delicious salad combines all the flavors of the Mediterranean. It is an excellent way of serving pasta and is particularly suitable for a hot summer day.

INGREDIENTS

Serves 6

1 pound short pasta, such as medium
    shells, farfalle or penne
4 tablespoons extra virgin olive oil
10 sun-dried tomatoes, thinly sliced
2 tablespoons capers, in brine or salted
1 cup pitted black olives
2 garlic cloves, finely chopped
3 tablespoons balsamic vinegar
3 tablespoons chopped fresh parsley
salt and ground black pepper

1 Cook the pasta in plenty of boiling salted water until *al dente.* Drain and rinse under cold water to stop the cooking. Drain well and turn into a large bowl. Toss with the olive oil and set aside until required.

2 Soak the tomatoes in a bowl of hot water for 10 minutes. Do not discard the water. Rinse the capers well. If they have been preserved in salt, soak them in a little hot water for 10 minutes. Rinse again.

3 Combine the olives, tomatoes, capers, garlic and vinegar in a small bowl. Season with salt and ground black pepper.

4 Stir the olive mixture into the cooked pasta and toss well. Add 2–3 tablespoons of the tomato soaking water if the salad seems too dry. Toss with the parsley and let stand for 15 minutes before serving.

Pasta, Melon and Shrimp Salad

Orange cantaloupe or Charentais melon look spectacular in this salad. Or try a mixture of ogen, cantaloupe and water melon.

Serves 4–6

6 ounces pasta shapes

2 cups frozen shrimp, thawed and drained

1 large or 2 small melons

4 tablespoons olive oil

1 tablespoon tarragon vinegar

2 tablespoons chopped fresh chives or chopped parsley

shredded Chinese leaves, to serve

herb sprigs, to garnish

1 Cook the pasta in boiling salted water according to the instructions on the package. Drain well, rinse and let cool.

2 Shell the shrimp and discard the shells.

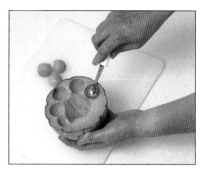

3 Halve the melon and remove the seeds with a teaspoon. Carefully scoop the flesh into balls with a melon baller and mix with the shrimp and pasta.

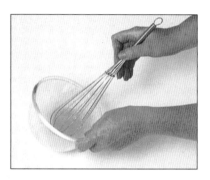

4 Whisk the oil, vinegar and chopped herbs together. Pour onto the shrimp mixture and turn to coat. Cover and chill for at least 30 minutes.

5 Meanwhile, shred the Chinese leaves and use to line a shallow bowl or the empty melon halves.

6 Pile the shrimp mixture onto the Chinese leaves and garnish with sprigs of herbs.

Roquefort and Walnut Pasta Salad

This is a simple, earthy salad, relying totally on the quality of the ingredients. There is no real substitute for Roquefort – a blue-veined ewe's-milk cheese which comes from southwest France.

INGREDIENTS

Serves 4

8 ounces pasta shapes

mixed salad leaves, such as arugula, curly endive, lamb's lettuce, baby spinach, radicchio

2 tablespoons walnut oil

4 tablespoons sunflower oil

2 tablespoons red wine vinegar or sherry vinegar

8 ounces Roquefort cheese, crumbled

1 cup walnut halves

salt and ground black pepper

1 Cook the pasta in plenty of boiling salted water, according to the instructions on the package. Drain well, rinse in cold water and let cool. Wash and dry the salad leaves and place in a large bowl.

COOK'S TIP

Try toasting the walnuts under the broiler for a couple of minutes to release the flavor.

2 Whisk together the walnut oil, sunflower oil, vinegar and salt and pepper to taste.

3 Pile the pasta in the center of the leaves, sprinkle the crumbled Roquefort over the top and pour on the dressing.

4 Sprinkle the walnuts over. Toss just before serving.

Whole Wheat Pasta Salad

This substantial vegetarian salad is easily assembled from any combination of seasonal vegetables. Use raw or lightly blanched vegetables, or a mixture of both.

Serves 8

1 pound short whole wheat pasta, such as fusilli or penne

3 tablespoons olive oil

2 carrots

1 small bunch broccoli

1½ cups shelled peas, fresh or frozen

1 red or yellow bell pepper

2 celery stalks

4 scallions

1 large tomato

¾ cup pitted olives

1 cup diced Cheddar or mozzarella cheese, or a combination of both

salt and ground black pepper

For the dressing

3 tablespoons white wine or balsamic vinegar

4 tablespoons olive oil

1 tablespoon Dijon mustard

1 tablespoon sesame seeds

2 teaspoons chopped mixed fresh herbs, such as parsley, thyme and basil

1 Cook the pasta in plenty of boiling salted water until *al dente*. Drain, and rinse under cold water to stop the cooking. Drain well and turn into a large bowl. Toss with 3 tablespoons of the olive oil and set aside. Let the pasta cool completely.

2 Lightly blanch the carrots, broccoli and peas in a large pan of boiling water. Refresh under cold water. Drain well.

3 Chop the carrots and broccoli into bite-size pieces and add to the pasta with the peas. Slice the bell pepper, celery, scallions and tomato into small pieces. Add them to the salad with the olives.

4 Make the dressing in a small bowl by combining the vinegar with the oil and mustard. Stir in the sesame seeds and herbs. Mix the dressing into the salad. Taste for seasoning, adding salt, pepper or more olive oil and vinegar, if necessary. Stir in the cheese, then let the salad stand for about 15 minutes before serving.

Smoked Trout Pasta Salad

Fennel bulb gives this salad a lovely anise flavor.

Serves 6

1 tablespoon butter

4 ounces ground fennel bulb

6 scallions, 2 ground and
   4 thinly sliced

8 ounces skinless smoked trout
   fillets, flaked

3 tablespoons chopped fresh dill

½ cup mayonnaise

2 teaspoons fresh lemon juice

2 tablespoons whipping cream

1 pound small pasta shapes, such as shells

salt and ground black pepper

fresh dill sprigs, to garnish

2 Add the sliced scallions, trout, dill, mayonnaise, lemon juice and cream. Mix gently until well blended.

3 Cook the pasta in plenty of boiling salted water, according to the instructions on the package, until *al dente*. Drain thoroughly, rinse in cold water and let cool.

4 Add the pasta to the vegetable and trout mixture and toss to coat evenly. Taste for seasoning and adjust if necessary. Serve the salad lightly chilled or at room temperature, garnished with dill.

1 Melt the butter in a small nonstick frying pan. Add the fennel and ground scallions and season lightly with salt and black pepper. Cook over medium heat for 3–5 minutes, or until just softened. Transfer to a large bowl and let cool slightly.

Artichoke Pasta Salad

Broccoli and black olives add color to this delicious salad.

INGREDIENTS

Serves 4

7 tablespoons olive oil

1 red bell pepper, quartered, seeded, and thinly sliced

1 onion, halved and thinly sliced

1 teaspoon dried thyme

3 tablespoons sherry vinegar

1 pound pasta shapes, such as penne or fusilli

2 x 6-ounce jars marinated artichoke hearts, drained and thinly sliced

5 ounces cooked broccoli, chopped

20–25 salt-cured black olives, pitted and chopped

2 tablespoons chopped fresh parsley

salt and ground black pepper

1 Heat 2 tablespoons of the olive oil in a nonstick frying pan. Add the red bell pepper and onion and cook over low heat until just soft, about 8–10 minutes, stirring from time to time.

2 Stir in the thyme, ¼ teaspoon salt and the vinegar. Cook, stirring, for 30 seconds more, then set aside.

3 Cook the pasta in plenty of boiling salted water, according to the instructions on the package, until *al dente.* Drain, rinse with hot water, then drain again. Transfer to a large bowl. Add 2 tablespoons of the oil and toss well to coat.

4 Add the artichokes, broccoli, olives, parsley, onion mixture and remaining oil to the pasta, and season. Stir to blend. Let stand for at least 1 hour before serving or chill overnight. Serve the salad at room temperature.

Pasta and Beet Salad

Color is vital at a party table, and this salad is certainly eye-catching. Prepare the egg and avocado at the last moment to avoid discoloration.

Serves 8

2 uncooked beets, scrubbed

8 ounces pasta shells or twists

3 tablespoons vinaigrette dressing

2 celery stalks, thinly sliced

3 scallions, sliced

¾ cup walnuts or hazelnuts,
    coarsely chopped

1 eating apple, cored, halved and sliced

salt and ground black pepper

For the dressing

4 tablespoons mayonnaise

3 tablespoons plain yogurt or
    ricotta cheese

2 tablespoons milk

2 teaspoons horseradish

To serve

curly lettuce leaves

3 eggs, hard-boiled and chopped

2 ripe avocados

1 box salad cress

1 Boil the beets, without peeling, in lightly salted water until they are just tender, about 1 hour. Drain, let cool, then peel and chop. Set aside.

2 Cook the pasta in plenty of boiled salted water according to the instructions on the package. Drain, toss in the vinaigrette and season well. Let cool, then mix with the beets, celery, scallions, nuts and apple in a bowl.

3 Stir all the dressing ingredients together and then mix into the pasta. Chill well.

4 To serve, line a salad bowl with the lettuce and spoon in the salad. Sprinkle the chopped egg over the top. Peel and slice the avocados and arrange them on top, then sprinkle on the cress.

Tuna Pasta Salad

This easy pasta salad uses canned beans and tuna for a quick main course dish.

Serves 6–8

1 pound short pasta, such as macaroni or
    farfalle

4 tablespoons olive oil

2 x 7-ounce cans tuna, drained
    and flaked

2 x 14-ounce cans cannellini or borlotti
    beans, rinsed and drained

1 small red onion

2 celery stalks

juice of 1 lemon

2 tablespoons chopped fresh parsley

salt and ground black pepper

1 Cook the pasta in plenty of boiling salted water until *al dente*. Drain, and rinse under cold water to stop the cooking. Drain well and turn into a large bowl. Toss with the olive oil and set aside. Let cool completely.

2 Mix the flaked tuna and the beans into the cooked pasta. Slice the onion and celery very thinly and add them to the pasta.

3 Combine the lemon juice with the parsley. Mix into the other ingredients. Season with salt and pepper. Let the salad stand for at least 1 hour before serving.

Chicken Pasta Salad

This salad uses leftover chicken from a roast or a cold poached chicken breast, if you prefer.

Serves 4

12 ounces short pasta, such as mezze,
    rigatoni, fusilli or penne

3 tablespoons olive oil

8 ounces cold cooked chicken

2 small red and yellow bell peppers

½ cup pitted green olives

4 scallions, chopped

3 tablespoons mayonnaise

1 teaspoon Worcestershire sauce

1 tablespoon white wine vinegar

salt and ground black pepper

a few fresh basil leaves, to garnish

1 Cook the pasta in plenty of boiling salted water until *al dente*. Drain, and rinse under cold water to stop the cooking. Drain well and turn into a large bowl. Toss with the olive oil and set aside. Let cool completely.

2 Cut the chicken into bite-size pieces, removing any bones. Cut the peppers into small pieces.

3 Combine all the ingredients except the pasta in a bowl. Taste for seasoning, then mix into the pasta. Serve well chilled, garnished with basil leaves.

DESSERTS

Strawberry Conchiglie Salad

A divinely decadent dessert laced with cherry liqueur and luscious raspberry sauce.

INGREDIENTS

Serves 4

6 ounces dried conchiglie

1⅓ cups raspberries, thawed if frozen

1–2 tablespoons superfine sugar

lemon juice

1 pound small fresh strawberries

slivered almonds

3 tablespoons kirsch

salt

1 Cook the pasta in a large saucepan of lightly salted, boiling water for 8–10 minutes, until tender, but still firm to the bite. Drain well and set aside to cool completely.

2 Purée the raspberries in a food processor and rub through a strainer. Put the purée and sugar in a small saucepan and simmer, stirring occasionally, for 5–6 minutes. Stir in lemon juice to taste and set aside to cool.

3 Hull the strawberries and cut in half if large. Toss with the pasta and transfer to a serving bowl.

4 Spread out the almonds on a cookie sheet and toast under the broiler until golden, then cool.

5 Stir the kirsch into the raspberry sauce and pour it over the salad. Scatter the toasted almonds on top and serve.

Dark Chocolate Ravioli

This is a spectacular chocolate pasta, with unsweetened cocoa added to the flour. The pasta packets contain a sumptuous white chocolate and cream cheese filling.

INGREDIENTS

Serves 4

1½ cups all-purpose white flour

¼ cup unsweetened cocoa

2 tablespoons confectioners' sugar

2 large eggs

light cream and grated chocolate, to serve

For the filling

6 ounces white chocolate

1½ cups cream cheese

2 eggs

1 Make the pasta dough following the instructions in the Introduction, but sift the flour with the unsweetened cocoa and confectioners' sugar before adding the eggs. Cover and set aside to rest for at least 30 minutes.

2 For the filling, break up the white chocolate and melt it in a bowl standing over a pan of barely simmering water. Cool slightly, then beat in the cream cheese and 1 egg. Spoon into a pastry bag fitted with a plain tip.

3 Cut the pasta dough in half and wrap one portion in plastic wrap. Roll the dough out thinly to a rectangle on a lightly floured surface, or use a pasta machine to roll out thinly. Cover with a clean, damp dish cloth and repeat with the remaining pasta dough.

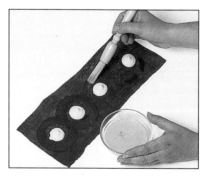

4 Pipe small mounds of the chocolate and cream cheese filling in even rows, spacing them at 1½-inch intervals, across one piece of the dough. Beat the remaining egg and lightly brush the spaces of dough between the mounds with it.

5 Using a rolling pin, lift the remaining sheet of pasta over the dough with the filling. Press down firmly between the pockets of filling, pushing out any trapped air. Cut into rounds with a serrated ravioli cutter or a sharp knife. Transfer to a floured dish cloth and set aside to rest for 1 hour.

6 Bring a large pan of lightly salted water to a boil and add the ravioli, a few at a time, stirring to prevent them from sticking together. Simmer gently for about 3–5 minutes, remove with a slotted spoon, and serve with light cream and grated chocolate.

Apple and Rhubarb Noodle Pudding

This is delicious hot or cold. The richness is offset by the tart flavors of apple and rhubarb.

INGREDIENTS

Serves 4–6

2 ounces dried short-cut macaroni

4 tablespoons butter

2 tablespoons light brown sugar

2 cooking apples, peeled, cored, and cut into eight

8 ounces rhubarb, cut into 1-inch lengths

pinch of ground cinnamon

½ cup cream cheese

½ cup superfine sugar

2 eggs

1 cup heavy cream

few drops of vanilla extract

pinch of grated nutmeg

confectioners' sugar, for dusting

1 Preheat the oven to 350°F. Grease one or two ovenproof dishes with a little butter. Melt the remaining butter in a skillet, add the brown sugar, and stir until it dissolves. Add the apples and rhubarb, stirring to coat. Sprinkle the cinnamon into the skillet and cook for 3–5 minutes.

2 Meanwhile, cook the macaroni in a saucepan of boiling water for 8–10 minutes, until tender, but still firm to the bite. Drain, rinse under cold water, and drain again.

3 In a bowl, beat the cream cheese, superfine sugar and eggs together until smooth. Stir in the cream and vanilla and mix well. Fold in the macaroni and the fruit mixture, then spoon the mixture into the prepared dishes.

4 Sprinkle the nutmeg over the top. Set the dishes in a roasting pan, then pour hot water into the pan to the depth of 1 inch. Bake for about 35 minutes, until set. Dust with confectioners' sugar and serve hot or cold.

Pasta Timbales with Apricot Sauce

Orzo or rice-shaped pasta inspired this dessert made like a rice pudding, but with a difference! Other small soup pasta can be used if orzo cannot be found.

INGREDIENTS

Serves 4

4 ounces dried orzo or other
    soup pasta
½ cup superfine sugar
2 tablespoons butter
1 vanilla bean, split
3⅔ cups milk
1¼ cups ready-made custard
3 tablespoons kirsch
1 tablespoon powdered gelatin
oil, for greasing
14 ounce can apricots
    in juice
lemon juice
salt
fresh flowers, to decorate (optional)

1 Place the orzo or other pasta, the sugar, a pinch of salt, the butter, vanilla bean and milk in a heavy-based saucepan and bring to a boil. Lower the heat and simmer, stirring frequently, for about 25 minutes until the pasta is tender and most of the liquid has been absorbed.

2 Remove and discard the vanilla bean and transfer the pasta to a bowl to cool completely. Then stir in the custard and 2 tablespoons of the kirsch.

3 Sprinkle the gelatin over 3 tablespoons water in a small bowl. Set the bowl in a pan of barely simmering water. Allow to become spongy and heat gently to dissolve. Stir it into the pasta in a thin continuous stream.

4 Lightly oil 4 timbale molds and spoon in the pasta. Refrigerate for 2 hours, until set.

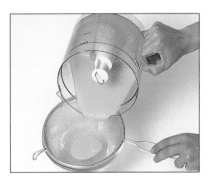

5 Meanwhile, purée the apricots in a food processor and then rub through a strainer. Stir in lemon juice to taste and the remaining kirsch.

6 Loosen the timbales from their molds and turn out onto plates. Spoon some apricot sauce around them and serve, decorated with fresh flowers, if desired.

Index